C O N T E N T S

THE COTTAGE GARDEN, THEN AND NOW   4
The Cottage Garden Evolves • The Cottage Garden
Essence—and Variations

THE ADAPTABLE COTTAGE GARDEN   12
The Basic Components of Climate • Climate Modifiers

PLANNING A COTTAGE GARDEN   22
Planning from Scratch • Effective Plant Combinations
Planning a Makeover • Inspirations • Routine Garden Care

A POTPOURRI OF FAVORITE COTTAGE GARDEN PLANTS   40
Annuals • Biennials • Perennials • Shrubs • Vines • Trees

SPECIALTY PLANTS TO COMPLETE THE PICTURE   78
Herbs • Ornamental Grasses • Vegetables & Fruits • Roses

DETAILS AND ACCESSORIES   102
Pathways • Fences, Walls, and Hedges • Gates • Tripods, Arches,
and Arbors • Trellises • Seating • Containers • Sundials
Bird Feeders, Baths, and Houses • Garden Art

CLIMATE ZONES AND MAPS   122

Index   127

CHAPTER ONE

THE  COTTAGE GARDEN, THEN AND NOW

A cottage garden… The words are intensely evocative, conjuring an image of a country lane where a charmingly unpretentious home— probably festooned with climbing roses—nestles in a frothy patch of flowers. Fortunately, such gardens are more than fantasies found only in paintings, movies, and the imagination: they actually do exist. Moreover, they're within the grasp of anyone with a house, a plot of land, and a sense of adventure. With just a modicum of planning, you can fashion a cottage garden from scratch or retool a humdrum patch into a flowery extravaganza. As you create your plan, you may find it helpful to know how such gardens developed and to think about the factors that inspired their design.

This lively garden is a perfect embodiment of the cottage garden style, beautifully complementing a quaint Victorian-era home. The planting has a relaxed, planned-by-Nature air, featuring a little of this, a little of that in strictly random assortment. The plants include white Siberian iris and campanula, cerise sweet William, and yellow-and-red columbine.

Here's an English cottage on a grand scale—an ideal, expansive "display case" for a riot of climbing roses. The blue delphiniums in the foreground are another cottage garden classic, a traditional choice wherever summers are relatively mild and the air is often cool and moist.

In their lush celebration of color, form, and fragrance, the flower-filled cottage gardens we admire today are a far cry from their medieval English forebears. In those first peasant plots, the focus was on utility, not beauty: the plants included primarily vegetables and fruits for eating, as well as a few herbs for scent and the simplest of home remedies.

Practicality determined the layout, too. A typical arrangement featured a straight path from public way to cottage door, with plants arrayed on either side. Herbs were planted near the cottage, while vegetables and small fruits such as raspberries grew in patches close to the path; any fruit or nut trees were set farther back, behind the pathway plants. Within this framework, though, organization was loose: plants were fitted in where space

Antique accents like this stone birdbath nicely suit the cottage garden spirit.

was available. A rude fence often surrounded the entire garden, offering protection from damage by livestock.

THE COTTAGE GARDEN EVOLVES

With the cultural changes of the Renaissance, the cottage plot gradually lost its purely practical focus and began the transformation into its present-day form—a garden intended more to delight the eye than stock the pantry. One of these changes was religious reformation. The break between the English monarchy and the Catholic church led to the dissolution of all the monasteries in England, and with these establishments gone, cottagers lost what had been the primary source of a wide range of medicinal herbs. They were thus forced to grow these plants, some of them highly decorative, at home—and over time, the ornamental qualities came to be valued far more than the therapeutic ones. Common yarrow (Achillea millefolium) and wood betony (Stachys officinalis) are two such plants, still treasured by cottage gardeners today.

A second influence was what we might now call a trend toward globalization. Contact among European countries increased; daring voyages intended to reach the Far East instead discovered the Americas. New plants soon arrived in England from both the continent and the New World. Some of these were strictly ornamental, among them spider flower (Cleome hasslerana) and the pinks and carnations (Dianthus). Others were useful; still others were both beautiful and useful, such as wormwood (Artemisia absinthium)

A look out the front door captures the colorful jumble that is the hallmark of cottage gardening: all the plants seem to jostle each other for space, spilling out onto the pathway. An openwork fence bedecked with flowering vines encloses the garden; a leafy arbor leads outside.

and the familiar sunflower (*Helianthus annuus*). And ultimately, many of these plants found their way into cottage gardens.

The move toward purely pretty cottage garden plants also gained impetus from the flourishing trade that accompanied early globalization. Trade increased England's prosperity overall—even among the lower classes, allowing them the luxury of adding a few plants chosen just for beauty to their plots of edibles and herbs.

Mantled with fragrant roses, its threshold softened by lavishly blooming lavender and geraniums, this cottage door extends a gracious welcome.

The following centuries saw garden fashions come and go on grand estates, but the humble cottage garden continued to thrive, including ever more flowering plants as the years rolled by. And when the Industrial Revolution produced a class of wealthy industrialists who looked to the unspoiled countryside for respite from the city's grime, these gardens were "discovered" by a cultural elite.

Through the 19th and early 20th centuries, the cottage garden landscape style became more defined, though by no means hard-and-fast—a flexibility that still holds true today. An explosion of plant discoveries and developments, a rise in the nursery trade, greater reliance on purchased produce (with a corresponding decline in the need for home-grown edibles)—all of these factors transformed the original small, utilitarian fenced plot into a brilliant showcase for flowers, foliage, and fragrance.

THE COTTAGE GARDEN ESSENCE—AND VARIATIONS

A thriving cottage garden is the picture of random exuberance: the plants seem to have sprung up naturally, jostling one another for space in a kaleidoscope of color. The truly successful cottage garden, though, does have some loose organization—and its carefree appearance also involves several design elements. The factors to consider (all of them allowing the gardener a fair amount of latitude) are layout,

An inviting pathway cuts directly through varied, eye-catching plantings. The path has an organized structure, featuring on-end squares defined by lines of bricks—but the look is still casual, thanks to the variously sized stones and pebbles that fill in the squares.

color, and use of garden ornaments and amenities. In each of these areas, you can opt for tradition or choose to depart a bit from the classical model. The photographs on these pages show you several approaches—all different, yet all unmistakably cottage style.

GARDEN LAYOUT As codified a century or more ago, the cottage garden's traditional design holds fairly close to the original medieval plan. You enter through a gate and move straight to the front door, following a path with edges softened by borders of flowers and foliage. Variations on the theme have become common, though: as long as the plantings capture the joyous cottage essence, you can achieve the feeling you're after with such nontraditional elements as curved paths, grass walkways, and sloping sites. You can even have a cottage garden entirely without the cottage! Indeed, two of the most renowned English estate gardens—Sissinghurst Castle and Hidcote Manor— offer examples of cottage-inspired plantings in the most elegant of settings, with nary a rustic dwelling in sight.

COLOR When it comes to color coordination, you can abandon all the rules, if you please! There's no one "correct" color tradition. As the original gardens evolved to include more ornamentals, the just-for-show plants were simply plugged in where room could be found for them. Riotous clashes could and did occur, but they were scarcely noticed amid the overall chromatic luxuriance. If you prefer to create a restful all-pastel planting, however, go right ahead.

Some gardeners have noted an interesting link between the evolution of garden plants and the effect of vivid colors. Among old-fashioned varieties and wild species, strong colors—even clashing ones—can assort without seeming "off." Modern hybrids in strident colors, on the other hand, are often rather stiff

Stone troughs are the ultimate in natural-looking containers, well suited to shallow-rooted plants.

plants, and the combination of stiff habit and strong color produces an artificial, plastic appearance. Such plants tend to look out of character in the relaxed, tousled array of a cottage garden.

AMENITIES AND ORNAMENTATION As the cottage plot shifted its focus from pure function toward beauty of form, it quite naturally became something

to admire and contemplate. The original amenity was thus a simple bench—a vantage point for viewing as well as a place to rest after a spell of hard work. Traditionally, the bench was positioned just outside the front door; at the peasant-farmer level, it would have been a no frills, rough-hewn wooden affair, though today's choices vary from rustic to more refined.

Like the garden bench, other forms of modern ornamentation also have a functional past. Arbors and trellises, now so often seen draped with roses, wisteria, clematis, and the like, would in olden times have accommodated beans, grapes, and various other vining edibles. (In the contemporary cottage garden, you'll often find such plant-training aids used for both edibles and ornamentals.)

LEFT *This planting, one of many at Sissinghurst Castle, is pure cottage style—if you overlook the castle turrets in the background!* **CENTER** *A simple packed-earth pathway harks back to original cottagers' plots.* **RIGHT** *This storybook garden follows the traditional layout, with a path running directly from gate to front door.*

A contemporary adaptation of the classic style, this garden captures the cottage essence with its bright, casual mixed plantings. There's a departure from tradition as well, though——the meandering turf grass pathway.

Containers, though something of a latter-day addition, nicely fit the mood if suitably "countrified." They look most natural when placed near the house—perhaps beside the garden bench. The basic terra-cotta pot, available in several sizes, is timeless and unshowy, always simple enough to fit in. Old stone troughs (and modern concrete-based re-creations of them) are the ultimate in country-cottage containers, and even an old bucket can be given new life as a rustic plant pot. But avoid anything too polished or elegant: Italianate urns, glazed ceramic pots, elaborately constructed wooden planters. Steer clear of kitsch such as worn-out boots or old pedestal sinks, too.

To explore the wide array of variations, from paths and fences to sundials and birdbaths, see the chapter on details and accessories (page 102).

CHAPTER TWO

THE ADAPTABLE COTTAGE GARDEN

You can be sure that the cottage gardens of old were maintained with a minimum of fuss. Natural predators provided pest control; rainfall was the watering mainstay. The only fertilizers available were animal manures and compost. Plants content with that level of culture and suited to the climate flourished, while those not so well adapted languished, died, or were crowded out by their more successful neighbors. Thus, the exuberant botanical hodgepodge characteristic of those original gardens was a tough, undemanding bunch. That point underscores the key to successful cottage gardening: for best results, choose plants that thrive under local conditions. Though you certainly can use fertilizers, pesticides, and supplemental water to improve performance, you cannot ignore or completely outwit your climate. Don't struggle against it: instead, learn to work with what it has to offer.

The Midwest flowering year begins with old-fashioned spring-blooming favorites, including pink peonies, purple and yellow irises, and hardy climbing roses. After the blossoms fade, the foliage provides a green foil for an even bigger display of summer-flowering perennials.

Tucked into a tousled array of flowers and grasses, a countrified bentwood chair offers a secluded retreat at the end of a trail of stepping–stones. The setting is Southern California, where red penstemon, white boltonia (an aster relative), and fountain grass thrive with little winter chill.

The English cottage garden developed in climates much like those found in parts of the Pacific Northwest and Northern California. In these areas, you can create classic English-style plantings brimming with everything that revels in relatively mild winters and cool to moderate, just slightly humid summers: delphiniums, campanulas, roses, lupine, and dozens more.

Remember, though, that cottage gardening is a *general* style, not one that requires a specific set of plants—and this means it's accessible for gardeners in a range of climates, as you'll see on these pages.

THE BASIC COMPONENTS OF CLIMATE

Mention climate, and temperature is usually the first thing that comes to mind. But there's more to climate than simple heat and cold. Though temperature (especially annual highs and lows) certainly plays an important role in plant adaptation and survival, rainfall and atmospheric moisture are also crucial in creating any region's climate.

TEMPERATURE As you design your garden, think first about the typical temperature extremes in your region. Some plants revel in blazing heat, while others prefer cool to mild summers. At the lower end of the scale, winter weather that dips just below freezing (32°F/0°C) will wipe

Summer in a Santa Fe high desert garden brings a surprisingly lavish floral array. The display is varied and crowded—yet each plant stands out from its neighbors, thanks to careful attention to color combinations and thoughtful arrangement of plant, leaf, and flower shapes and sizes.

A Northeastern midsummer features fragrant cerise 'Apothecary's Rose' (R. gallica 'Officinalis') framed by the classic duo of white ox-eye daisy (Chrysanthemum leucanthemum) and yellow fernleaf yarrow. Silvery gray lamb's ears and yellow-dotted lavender cotton grow in the foreground.

out tender plants, while more rugged individuals can comfortably endure weeks or months of temperatures far below that threshold.

A region's annual hot-and-cold patterns define its *growing season:* the number of days between the usual last freeze (in winter or spring) and the first frost of fall or winter. In mild-winter regions, the growing season can last almost all year. But where frosts come early and temperatures are subfreezing for long stretches, the season is attenuated. In these regions, be sure to choose flowers and vegetables that will mature within the frost-free period.

In general, the growing season is longer at lower latitudes (closer to the equator) and becomes progressively shorter as you move north or south toward the poles. (As some compensation for their shorter growing season, high-latitude areas have more hours of sunlight each day during the season than low-latitude regions do.) Altitude also has an influence: the higher the elevation, the shorter the growing season. Mountain gardens have cooler summer temperatures as well—so gardeners there must opt for fast-maturing plants that also prefer moderate weather during summer.

RAINFALL The luxury of being able to turn on a tap and send water to the garden makes the issue of natural rainfall less important than it once was. Even so, where water is naturally scarce during the growing season (or is limited in availability then), it's best to seek out less-thirsty plants. You can craft surprisingly luxuriant cottage-style gardens from such plants, thus freeing yourself from the tyranny of a regular watering schedule.

HUMIDITY The moisture content of air ranges from nearly zero—the desiccating dryness of desert regions—to the saturated, almost liquid atmosphere of a fogbound coast. This moisture content is not linked to temperature: dry air can be desert-hot or bracingly cool (as it is in the mountains), and in addition to the damp chill of fog there is, of course, the steam-bath summer humidity of many lowland regions east of the Rockies. Many favorite cottage garden plants tolerate varying degrees of humidity, but some are quite particular.

CLIMATE MODIFIERS
Though the basics just discussed—annual temperature patterns, rainfall, and humidity—define a region's essential

WHY IS SUMMER THAT WAY?

Hot, cool, humid, dry... across the United States and Canada, the quality of summer weather stems from a combination of geography, ocean winds and currents, and atmospheric conditions.

If they're high enough, mountain ranges play a key role in determining weather by blocking and directing influences from the Atlantic and Pacific oceans and the Gulf of Mexico. In North America, the West's high mountains fall into this category—the Sierra Nevada/Cascade coastal axis, running from British Columbia to southern California, and the Rocky Mountains, which extend from within Canada south into central Mexico. Pacific Ocean dominance tends to remain west of the Sierra Nevada/Cascade ranges, while influences from the Atlantic and the Gulf of Mexico are primarily felt east of the Rockies. (The generally lower Appalachian ranges in the East, in contrast, have comparatively little effect on weather.)

In the ocean, warm currents flow through the Gulf of Mexico and (as the well-known Gulf Stream) move up the Atlantic coast. During summer, these currents affect the entire eastern seaboard: the warm water evaporates readily, resulting in humid air. The Pacific coastal area, on the other hand, is washed by cold southward-moving currents that travel nearly to Mexico. Because cold water evaporates much less readily than warm water does, Pacific Coast air is relatively dry.

In the atmosphere, semipermanent areas of high pressure that generally lie offshore hover over the tropics in winter. In summer, though, they migrate northward, reaching a latitude about the same as that of Philadelphia, Pennsylvania, in the East and Eureka, California, in the West. The juxtaposition of high pressure offshore and lower pressure over land generates winds that blow toward land. In the West, relatively cool, dry air moves inland off the ocean; near the coast, coolness is the general rule, but farther inland, conditions are dry and hot. In the eastern part of the continent, the air that comes onshore is warm and moist, spawning summer rainfall and generally muggy weather.

In addition, warm, moist air from the Gulf of Mexico moves north and northeast, affecting land from the Midwest to the Atlantic seaboard (the influence diminishes as you move north). Periodically, colder air masses originating in the North Atlantic move south and west over land and meet the warmer air. In the eastern United States and Canada, such cold-warm collisions usually produce cooler temperatures and drizzle. Over the midsection of the continent, though, the results can be much more dramatic: spectacular thunderstorms, heavy rains, even tornadoes.

Between the Sierra Nevada/Cascade and Rocky Mountain ranges lies the Great Basin, a semiarid to arid "rain shadow" region. In summer, Pacific influence there is blocked from the west by the Sierra Nevada/Cascade mountains, while the Rockies keep out moisture moving northward from the Gulf of Mexico. The result is summers that are both dry and hot.

Two Pacific Coast gardens illustrate different planting styles. **LEFT** *A Northern California cottage features an eclectic floral mix spilling onto a meandering gravel pathway. An elaborate roofed feeder ensures frequent visits from birds.* **RIGHT** *Western Oregon offers the perfect climate for roses—and this garden takes advantage of it. The roses are fronted by low, spreading plants, among them a purple-flowered geranium.*

climate, the gardening picture is also influenced by other factors. Three of the most important such modifiers are wind, exposure, and the presence of nearby bodies of water.

WIND Whether they arrive daily or seasonally, regular winds affect climate. Near the ocean (especially on the Pacific Coast), moist on-shore winds are virtually an everyday occurrence. Directly at the shore, they buffet plants with salt-laden air that will damage all but particularly tolerant individuals. A bit farther inland, though, they're softer and not salty—yet they still deliver refreshing coolness, keeping temperatures lower than they are

even farther inland (and letting gardeners worry less about their plants' heat tolerance).

Especially across large parts of the Midwest, arid wind during

High in the Rocky Mountains, summer is brightened by varied perennials, here blooming among boulders and gray-trunked aspens.

the growing season is a fact of life and a force to be dealt with. Some plants stand up to it, while others wilt from its relentless drying effect.

In any region, windbreaks offer one option for coping with incessant winds. A simpler solution, though, is to select plants that thrive even when constantly blown to and fro.

EXPOSURE In both the larger geographic context and the smaller home-garden sphere, exposure influences the prevailing climate—and can greatly affect plant performance.

Exposure differences are especially pronounced in hilly and mountainous land. South-

Deep in the South, a weathered 18th-century home stands in a clearing amid a pine woodland. Featuring favorites such as roses, peonies, hollyhocks, and foxgloves, the cottage-style planting looks relaxed and casual, almost like a collection of wildflowers.

facing slopes get maximum sun exposure, often from dawn right through to sunset. This is the warmest exposure, with the longest interval between frosts. North-facing slopes, in contrast, are cooler in all seasons than south-facing ones; when the sun is low in winter, they can be entirely in shade, and even in summer they're likely to be shaded for part of the day. Northern exposures also warm up later in the year and cool down earlier, resulting in a somewhat shortened growing season. East-facing slopes receive morning sun but become shaded at some point in the afternoon; west-facing slopes experience the reverse situation, receiving afternoon sun when it

Summer has many faces. **TOP LEFT** *In a North Carolina garden, the accent is on warm-colored flowers that thrive in the humid climate.* **TOP RIGHT** *A Midwestern planting features foliage and flowers adapted to heat and dryness.* **BOTTOM LEFT** *The Alaskan summer is like an English spring—perfect for flowers that like it cool.* **BOTTOM RIGHT** *This riotous Iowa garden showcases a carefree assortment of breadbox poppies, native black-eyed Susans* (Rudbeckia), *magenta crown pinks, and yellow fernleaf yarrow.*

is most intense. In many regions, both south- and west-facing slopes can be brutally hot during summer's long days, making them best suited to less-thirsty, sun-worshipping plants.

During the winter months, slope matters in another way.

Warm air rises, while cold air sinks—so areas that are higher on slopes of any exposure are not as chilly as those located at the bottom of a hill or mountain. Land at the low end of a slope is also likely to stay colder for longer periods than that higher up.

In the home garden, be it on a sloping or totally flat plot, structures and trees create northern, eastern, southern, and western exposures with the characteristics just described. Knowing how your garden is oriented will guide your selection of

A Colonial-era picket fence defines the boundaries of this Atlantic seaboard cottage garden while still leaving it open to public view. The plantings nicely suit the historical theme, featuring many selections—such as white spider flowers and yellow daylilies—that would have been familiar to the colonists.

appropriate plants. Note, too, that gardeners on sloping land have an additional concern in winter: as cold air sinks to the lowest level, it "pools" on the uphill sides of structures, making these places (regardless of exposure) colder than the rest of the garden. A spot higher on a slope can thus actually be as cold as one lower down, since the structure has, so to speak, introduced a "false bottom" to the slope.

PROXIMITY OF WATER Substantial bodies of water, such as oceans and large lakes, have a moderating effect on tempera-ture. Because these waters warm up and cool down more slowly than land masses do, they exert a tempering influence on the land that borders them. On the coast and lakeside, winter weather is generally a bit warmer than that farther inland, while summer is a little milder.

THE SUNSET CLIMATE ZONES

Many of the plants you'll see in this book are described in more detail in the encyclopedia beginning on page 40. Each plant listed there is zoned according to *Sunset's* climate zone system, which organizes the contiguous 48 states, adjacent Canadian provinces, Alaska, and Hawaii into 53 different climatic regions. Zone maps and descriptions appear on pages 122–126.

Determine your zone from the maps; then, as you plan your garden, select plants that are known to be successful in that zone and that suit your particular conditions.

CHAPTER THREE

PLANNING A COTTAGE GARDEN

A carefully planned cottage garden? The phrase sounds almost contradictory. After all, the charm of a cottage garden is in its apparent lack of planning: plants jostle each other and spill over pathways with careless exuberance, seemingly unguided by a gardener's hand. Nonetheless, the most successful cottage gardens do have a basic structure, an underlying, firmly established framework within which random assortments and impulse planting can create carefree beauty, not mere chaos.

This cottage garden's ebullient looks belie the planning that went into creating the carefree effect. The gardener chose plants that suit the climate, then arranged them to complement and contrast with each other. And everything was positioned with ease of maintenance in mind.

Nestled in a landscape that fairly bubbles over with a varied assortment of flowers and foliage, this unpretentious wood-frame house and its garden make a perfect match: both are relaxed, informal, and inviting.

Like any other garden, a cottage garden can be created from scratch—on a previously unplanted patch of ground—or developed as a remodel of an existing garden.

In both cases, you're aiming to establish a bare-bones framework that can then be clothed in plants. The process is much the same in either instance, though of course the "bones" will be barer at the outset if you're starting from nothing; you won't have to make so many decisions about what to save, what to remove or replace.

PLANNING FROM SCRATCH

Like a blank page, an empty patch of land is entirely open to inspiration. It can be a little intimidating, though: where do you start? What should you include? A methodical approach to planning is the key to moving forward with confidence.

HOW MUCH GARDEN? First, decide how large your cottage garden should be. Will you devote your entire yard to it, or will part of the land be turned over to other needs? If you know, for example, that you simply must have a swimming pool and a croquet pitch, pick the locations for these first—and then see what remains for a garden.

If only part of the total garden will be in the cottage style, think about transitions from one area to another. A house or wall can successfully separate two distinctly different styles or uses; but lacking that, try for a linking structure, something to show that the entire garden, however varied, is a single unit.

A pathway or pergola leading out of the cottage garden creates a graceful transition; a flower-decked arbor also makes an attractive boundary.

At this point, it's wise to make a sketch of the area *to scale*. In

TOP It looks appropriately unfettered, but this back garden still has a plan: though the plantings draw the eye this way and that, the path keeps you moving toward the bench, a vantage point for surveying the entire scene. BOTTOM LEFT A straight path transects a front garden, taking the visitor directly from sidewalk to house. BOTTOM RIGHT Though it lacks a real yard, this two-story home still sports a front cottage garden—in containers.

avoiding planning pitfalls, nothing is as helpful as a reference that lets you make plans representing actual measure on the ground. Without a scale drawing as a guide, you're likely to think you can cram in many more plants than the space will actually hold.

ASSESS IMMOVABLE OBJECTS

Begin the planning process by locating and evaluating any permanent features within the area you've chosen. These include the house; outbuildings such as garden sheds or detached garages; walls and fences; and any pathways you plan to keep. Mark the locations of all these on your scale drawing. Also note down any trees that will remain in place.

After you've established what can't or won't be moved, think about where to site *new* permanent features. If you want walls, fences, or hedges, indicate their places on the plot plan. Then consider probable locations of pathways for getting through the area (just note the points they must connect; the final route won't necessarily be a straight line). With boundaries defined and basic circulation routes indicated, you can more clearly see where other permanent fixtures such as arbors, trellises, and benches might be placed to advantage.

MAP OUT PLANTING AREAS

Once you've completed the steps just described, you'll have a good idea of how much room will be left untouched for actual planting. If the overall space was fairly limited at the outset, you may find that the available area has been automatically reduced to practical planting bed size. The more challenging scenario, however, leaves you with larger expanses of bare ground—and thus more design options.

While it's true that the cottage garden look is one of exuberant excess, you don't want to saddle yourself with a jungly nightmare. Always plan with

Comfortably wide paths let border plants spill over the margins, while still leaving plenty of room for easy strolling—and for maintenance aids like wheelbarrows and tarpaulins. This graceful curved pathway is covered in wood chips for a clean, attractive surface.

LEFT *With thoughtful planning, plants can stand out individually but also fit nicely into the larger picture.* **RIGHT** *This varied and colorful planting is a stellar example of effective plant combination—and it shows how much can be grown in a bed narrow enough for easy maintenance.*

maintenance in mind. You want to get through the garden easily, and you'll also need to be able to get into the beds without machete and pith helmet!

Pathways are one key to easy maintenance, so start by firming up the routes of the paths you need. Make the major ones at least wide enough to accommodate a wheelbarrow (you'll probably need one to transport soil amendments into the area and to remove garden refuse from it). Broad paths also let you stroll through the garden with friends without having to walk single file.

Another requirement for easy maintenance is good planting bed design. Ideally, the plants farthest away from a path will still be within arm's reach. This translates to a bed width of 3½ to 4 feet where a path runs along just one side, 7 to 8 feet for a bed flanked by paths. If the beds are any wider than this, you'll have to wade into them for routine tidying. For the opulent look deeper beds can give, you can

build in discreet access points, such as well-placed stepping-stones or narrow walks that thread their way into the planting.

POSITION THE PLANTS
Determine the location of your permanent plants—trees, shrubs, vines, large ornamental grasses—before you select or plant anything else. These are likely to be the largest plants you'll install, so it's easier to set them in when nothing else is growing close by. And once they're in place, you can more clearly see what other plants might best serve as their immediate neighbors.

With permanent plants positioned and their approximate mature sizes noted on the plot plan, begin filling in around them with perennials and annuals, always being sure that you group together those with like cultural needs (sun lovers with sun lovers, thirsty types with other thirsty types, for instance). Resist the inevitable temptation to cram in

absolutely everything you want; instead, pay attention to each plant's eventual size (both height and spread) and allow each one enough room to develop well. Fairly close planting is fine—it produces the look you're after—but if plants are packed *too* tightly, the competition will keep them from growing as they should. What's more, too-close quarters offer a breeding ground for pests and diseases.

If you want tight control on the outcome, you can plan an exact arrangement, carefully observing the points covered in "Effective Plant Combinations" (page 28). To be true to the cottage garden spirit, however, just choose plants by whim, impulse, and opportunity, making sure only that your choices have the right size, shape, and cultural needs for the spot. If you've followed the previous planning and layout advice, either approach will yield a casual-looking, delightfully varied outcome.

EFFECTIVE PLANT COMBINATIONS

The flowery cottage gardens of old may have been randomly planted affairs, but that doesn't preclude the notion that at least some of the old cottagers had an artistic eye for arrangement. "Impulse" planting is just that, but you may never have the impulse to plant, say, an orange flower next to a magenta one! Here's a checklist of points you may want to consider as you assemble your planting.

PLANT SIZE It's old advice, but still valid: locate tall plants in the back of a bed, medium-size ones in the middle, short types in front. Particularly if the taller individuals are bulky, they look best at the back—or in the center, if the bed can be accessed and viewed from more than one side. There are exceptions, of course; some lofty plants (particularly upright, open-structured ones) can be moved forward singly to create a dramatic accent and focal point as they rise from amid their shorter neighbors.

PLANT SHAPE A look at a mixed garden or a trip to the nursery provides ample illustration of the enormous range of plant shapes: tall and straight or low and carpetlike; oval, fountain shaped,

Carefully designed beds, arranged with an eye toward plant sizes, shapes, colors, and foliage textures, can still look casual.

pyramidal, or rounded; upright, mounding, or spreading. The most dynamic plantings take advantage of all this variety in form.

FOLIAGE VARIETY
Even more varied than overall plant shapes are the shapes and sizes of foliage. Leaves can be feathery, fernlike, grassy, fan shaped, paddlelike, round, oval, and so on—and their sizes range from tiny to huge. What's more, plant size and leaf size don't always correspond. You'll find big plants with small, fine leaves; small ones with big, coarse leaves; bulky types with filmy foliage; and open, see-through plants with large

leaves. By freely combining foliage, you avoid any hint of monotony.

COLOR In most gardens, flower color is what strikes us first—and a cottage garden is your original riot of color. You can plant without giving color combinations much mind, leaving the door open for every imaginable contrast, harmony, and clash; or you can provide more guidance, choosing to plan out combinations and exclude some hues from the overall palette. Do remember, though, that flower size and floral density affect a color's impact: tiny, blazing red blossoms scattered here and there over a plant can go practically unnoticed in the neighborhood of a shrub that's smothered in huge pale pink flowers.

Foliage color plays a subtler but still valuable role in varying a planting. Basic green comes in a great range, including pale to dark pure greens as well as those tinged with blue, gray, or yellow. You'll also find many plants with foliage in gray, silver, steel blue, yellow, bronze, red, and purple. And don't forget variegated leaves; once you start looking, you'll be surprised to discover how many plants offer foliage combining two, three, or even more colors.

Garden makeovers can vary in scope. **LEFT** *A small front yard lends itself beautifully to a cottage-style planting.* **RIGHT** *On a more expansive scale, what could have been a monotonous expanse of grass is much more effective dressed up in a rambunctious assortment of flowers.*

PLANNING A MAKEOVER

Converting an existing garden to the cottage style is in many ways similar to starting from scratch. The most important difference is this: when you remodel, you'll have to spend much more time deciding what to keep and what to discard.

SCOPE IT OUT Decide how much of the garden you want to transform: backyard, front yard, entry walk, and so on. Once you've settled on the project area, prepare a scale drawing of it as described under "How much garden?" (page 24).

SORT IT OUT Though you're planning to create a new garden, there may well be elements of the old one you will want to retain—or will be forced to keep because removal is too much trouble. Start by considering structural features: existing pathways, fences, walls, gates, garden outbuildings, arbors, pergolas. Think about major plants, too; worthwhile trees, large hedges, and favorite specimen shrubs should be given a chance to shine in a new setting. On your scale drawing, indicate the locations of everything you want to (or have to) keep.

REFINE THE PLAN Now think about other permanent features you'd like to include, and see if they'll work with those already in place. Consider where you might want new boundaries (such as hedges or walls); plot out the best locations for pathways. As you work, you may discover that you'll need to part with more of the original garden than you'd first thought or aban-don some of the elements on your wish list—or just keep on rethinking locations. If that old lilac falls right in the middle of an ideal pathway route, for example, you may have to sacrifice (or move) it. If a favorite productive plum tree is growing on the very spot where a rose arbor would bring a perfect finishing touch to the cottage scene, you'll have to remove the tree, bid the arbor adieu, or preserve both by finding another, equally perfect location for the flowery arbor you long for.

PROCEED TO CONCLUSION Now that you have the basic framework in place, you're ready to fill things in. At this point, you can follow the guidelines noted earlier for gardens started from scratch, beginning with "Map out planting areas" (page 26).

Which came first—garden or gate? This planting is so naturalistically disheveled it's hard to tell if it was planned or not. Effects like this are easily achieved by using plants adapted to your climate. They grow with little attention—and many self-sow, all but ensuring a planted-at-random look.

INSPIRATIONS

In the previous pages, we've outlined the planning process, reviewing the factors to consider as you create the perfect design for your new cottage garden. In the next seven pages, you'll find a bit more help: three sample garden plans and six lists of plants to suit various locations or serve certain purposes (to fill a hot, sunny corner or attract butterflies, for example). Replicate one of the designs exactly, if you like—or simply use it as a starting point, choosing the features and the plants that fit your needs, then adding on from there.

The plans are simple to read. A watercolor illustration shows the garden at the peak of bloom; a plot plan shows the entire planting from above, with the area occupied by each plant labeled by a letter. These letters correspond to those in the accompanying plant list; the total number of each plant used is indicated in parentheses after that plant's name. To see where a plant fits into the design, just check for its letter on the plot plan. In our Flowery Nook (page 32), for example, letter U designates *Heuchera sanguinea*, commonly called coral bells. Looking at the plot plan, you can see that it's planted in two spots; checking the plant list, you'll see that we've used eight plants total, to be divided between these two locations.

HEAT-TOLERANT PLANTS

When the sun is blazing, plants can't escape into air-conditioned comfort. If you live where late spring and summer temperatures drive you indoors, you'll appreciate those tough plants that actually revel in heat, looking presentable even on blistering days.

Annuals

Cleome hasslerana. Zones 1–45
Coreopsis tinctoria. Zones 1–45, H1, H2
Cosmos bipinnatus. Zones A3, 1–45
Gomphrena globosa. Zones 1–45, H1, H2
Portulaca grandiflora. All zones
Salvia viridis. All zones
Verbena. All zones

Perennials

Achillea. Zones A1–A3, 1–24, 26, 28–45
Agastache. Zones vary
Asclepias tuberosa. Zones 1–45
Centranthus ruber. Zones 2–9, 12–24, 28–43, H1
Echinacea purpurea. Zones A2, A3, 1–24, 26–45

Shrubs

Buddleja davidii. Zones 2–24, 28–41, H1
Caryopteris × clandonensis. Zones 2b–9, 14–24, 29–41
Hibiscus syriacus. Zones 2–24, northern 26, 28–41, H1
Phlomis fruticosa. Zones 3b–24, 31, warmer 32

Trees

Lagerstroemia indica. Zones 6–10, 12–31, warmer 32, H1, H2

Ornamental grasses

Muhlenbergia. Zones vary
Panicum virgatum. Zones 1–11, 14–23, 28–43

Herbs

Artemisia (most). Zones vary
Santolina chamaecyparissus. Zones 2–24, 27, 29, 30, 32–35, 39, H1, H2
Teucrium chamaedrys. Zones 2–24, 28–41

Vegetables & fruits

Eggplant. All zones
Pepper. All zones
Sunflower. All zones

SHADE-TOLERANT PLANTS

A completely open location will receive full sun from dawn to sunset, but most planting beds are shaded to some degree by structures, trees, or large shrubs. Often, a bed that's bright and sunny for part of the day will be in shadow in the morning or afternoon—or early or late in the season, when the sun is lower in the sky. And trees growing near a bed may cast dappled shade on it during the middle of the day. In any location that's in shade for about half the day, the following plants will perform well.

Annuals

Gomphrena globosa. Zones 1–45, H1, H2
Myosotis sylvatica. Zones A1–A3, 1–24, 32–45
Nigella damascena. All zones
Viola. Zones vary

Biennials

Digitalis purpurea. Zones A2, A3, 1–24, 31–41
Erysimum. Zones vary

Perennials

Agastache. Zones vary
Anemone × hybrida. Zones 2b–24, 30–43
Aquilegia. Zones vary
Centranthus ruber. Zones 2–9, 12–24, 28–43, H1
Geranium. Zones vary
Lychnis. Zones vary
Primula. Zones vary
Stachys. Zones 1–24, 29–43
Viola odorata. Zones 1–24, 29–43

Vines

Clematis. Zones vary
Lonicera. Zones vary
Tropaeolum majus. All zones
Vitis. Zones vary
Wisteria sinensis. Zones 3–24, 26, 28–35, 37, 39

Shrubs

Buddleja. Zones vary
Deutzia. Zones 2–11, 14–17, 29–41
Kolkwitzia amabilis. Zones 2–11, 14–20, 31–41
Spiraea. Zones vary
Viburnum. Zones vary
Weigela. Zones 1–11, 14–21, 32–41

Trees

Cornus florida. Zones 2b–9, 14–16, northern 26, 28, 29, 31–41
Magnolia. Zones vary

Ornamental grasses

Most. Zones vary

Herbs

Hyssopus officinalis. Zones 1–24, 30–45
Prunella. Zones 2–24, 29–43

Vegetables & fruits

Chives. All zones

A FLOWERY NOOK

The spirit of a classic Victorian cottage garden reigns in this quiet corner. The bed has the traditional planted-at-random look—but in fact, each plant is placed where it will show to best advantage and harmonize with its neighbors. The garden spills over to the crazy-paving pathway, where spreading clumps of sweet alyssum bloom between the stones. A simple but elegant bench provides the perfect spot from which to appreciate this floral festival.

This scheme is best suited to Zones 2b–7, 14–16, 34, and 39. To expand it to Zones 8, 9, 17–20, 32, 33, 35–38, 40, and 41, replace the lavender (F in the plan) with blue mist (*Caryopteris × clandonensis*), the delphinium (K) with spider flower (*Cleome hasslerana*), and the lupine (L) with anise hyssop (*Agastache foeniculum*). The latter two substitutions are not truly equivalent to the plants they replace, but they're still consistent with the mood of the planting.

A. *Rosa* 'Cornelia' (1)

B. *Rosa* 'Ballerina' (1)

C. *Rosa* 'Iceberg' (1)

D. *Syringa vulgaris* 'President Lincoln'. Common lilac (1)

E. *Spiraea japonica* 'Anthony Waterer' (2)

F. *Lavandula angustifolia*. English lavender (4) OR *Caryopteris × clandonensis*. Blue mist (4) *

G. *Paeonia* 'Festiva Maxima'. Peony (3)

H. *Gypsophila paniculata* 'Perfecta'. Baby's breath (3)

I. *Foeniculum vulgare* 'Purpurascens'. Bronze fennel (1)

J. *Alcea rosea*, Chater's Double strain. Hollyhock (3)

K. *Delphinium elatum* 'Summer Skies' (7) OR *Cleome hasslerana*. Spider flower (7)*

L. *Lupinus*, Russell Hybrids. Lupine (3) OR *Agastache foeniculum*. Anise hyssop (3)*

M. *Achillea* 'Coronation Gold'. Yarrow (5)

N. *Chrysanthemum maximum* 'Alaska'. Shasta daisy (6)

O. *Campanula persicifolia* 'Telham Beauty'. Peach-leafed bluebell (5)

P. *Aster × frikartii* 'Mönch' (6)

Q. *Iris,* tall bearded, light yellow (7)

R. *Geranium sanguineum* (4)

S. *Scabiosa caucasica.* Pincushion flower (6)

T. *Euphorbia polychroma.* Cushion spurge (4)

U. *Heuchera sanguinea.* Coral bells (8)

V. *Dianthus plumarius.* Cottage pink (5)

W. *Sedum* 'Autumn Joy' (5)

X. *Lychnis coronaria.* Crown pink, mullein pink, rose campion (5)

Y. *Stachys byzantina* 'Silver Carpet'. Lamb's ears (5)

Z. *Aurinia saxatilis.* Basket-of-gold (4)

AA. *Lobularia maritima,* set among the crazy-paving. Sweet alyssum (12)

* Use the second choice listed if you live in Zones 8, 9, 17–20, 32, 33, 35–38, 40, or 41.

FRAGRANT FLOWERS

Without fragrance, even the loveliest garden is somehow lacking. And for cottage gardens, perfumed blossoms are a must— they're part of the romance. The following famously fragrant plants are all ideal choices.

Annuals
Lobularia maritima. All zones
Nicotiana (some). All zones
Reseda odorata. All zones
Scabiosa atropurpurea. Zones 1–45, H1, H2
Biennials
Erysimum. Zones vary
Perennials
Dianthus. Zones vary

Iberis sempervirens. Zones 1–24, 31–45
Iris (bearded). Zones 1–24, 30–45
Paeonia. Zones A1–A3, 1–11, 14–20, 30–45
Primula vulgaris. Zones A3, 2–6, 14–17, 21–24, 32–41
Viola odorata. Zones 1–24, 29–43
Vines
Lathyrus odoratus. All zones
Lonicera (some). Zones vary
Wisteria. Zones vary
Shrubs
Buddleja. Zones vary
Philadelphus (many). Zones vary
Rosa (see page 94). Zones vary
Syringa vulgaris. Zones A1–A3, 1–22, 32–45
Viburnum × carlcephalum. Zones 3–11, 14–24, 31–34, 39

SEED- AND FRUIT-BEARING PLANTS FOR BIRDS

Fruit-eating birds will flock to the vines and trees noted here; seed eaters find good food sources in the rest. (To attract seed-eating birds, you will need to leave some spent flowers in place, so they'll set and ripen seed.)

Annuals
Calendula officinalis. Zones 1–45, H1
Centaurea cyanus. Zones 1–45, H1; H2
Coreopsis tinctoria. Zones 1–45, H1, H2
Cosmos bipinnatus. Zones A3, 1–45
Eschscholzia californica. Zones 1–45, H1
Lobularia maritima. All zones
Nigella damascena. All zones
Scabiosa atropurpurea. Zones 1–45, H1, H2

Biennials
Digitalis purpurea. Zones A2, A3, 1–24, 31–41
Perennials
Aquilegia. Zones vary
Echinacea purpurea. Zones A2, A3, 1–24, 26–45
Vines
Lonicera. Zones vary
Vitis. Zones vary
Trees
Cornus florida. Zones 2b–9, 14–16, northern 26, 28, 29, 31–41
Crataegus. Zones vary
Prunus. Zones vary
Ornamental grasses
Most. Zones vary
Herbs
Lavandula. Zones vary
Vegetables & fruits
Sunflower. All zones

TOP Iris, *tall bearded.* **CENTER** Peony (Paeonia). **BOTTOM** *Sunflower* (Helianthus annuus).

PLANTS FOR BUTTERFLIES AND HUMMINGBIRDS

If you want your garden to attract butterflies and hummingbirds, be sure to include flowers that provide nectar for them. Listed below are a number of proven favorites.

Annuals

Antirrhinum majus. Zones A3, 1–45
Cleome hasslerana. Zones 1–45
Consolida ajacis. Zones 1–45
Lobularia maritima. All zones
Nicotiana. All zones
Scabiosa atropurpurea. Zones 1–45, H1, H2
Verbena. Zones vary

Biennials

Alcea rosea. Zones 1–45
Dianthus barbatus. Zones A2, A3, 1–24, 30–45
Digitalis purpurea. Zones A2, A3, 1–24, 31–41
Erysimum cheiri. Zones 4–6, 14–17, 22, 23, 32, 34

Perennials

Achillea. Zones A1–A3, 1–24, 26, 28–45
Agastache. Zones vary
Aquilegia. Zones vary
Asclepias tuberosa. Zones 1–45
Aster. Zones vary
Centranthus ruber. Zones 2–9, 12–24, 28–43, H1
Chrysanthemum maximum. Zones A1–A3, 1–24, northern 26, 28–43, H1
Delphinium elatum. Zones A1–A3, 1–10, 14–24, 32, 34, 36–41
Dianthus. Zones vary
Echinacea purpurea. Zones A2, A3, 1–24, 26–45
Heuchera. Zones vary
Iberis sempervirens. Zones 1–24, 31–45

Liatris spicata. Zones A2, A3, 1–10, 14–24, 26, 28–45
Lupinus. Zones A1–A3, 1–7, 14–17, 34, 36–45
Penstemon. Zones vary
Salvia. Zones 2–10, 14–24, 30–41
Scabiosa. Zones vary

Vines

Ipomoea. All zones
Lathyrus odoratus. All zones
Lonicera. Zones vary
Tropaeolum majus. All zones

Shrubs

Hibiscus syriacus. Zones 2–24, northern 26, 28–41, H1
Buddleja. Zones vary
Caryopteris × clandonensis. Zones 2b–9, 14–24, 29–41
Kolkwitzia amabilis. Zones 2–11, 14–20, 31–41
Philadelphus (single-flowered). Zones vary
Spiraea. Zones vary
Syringa vulgaris. Zones A1–A3, 1–22, 32–45
Weigela. Zones 1–11, 14–21, 32–41

Herbs

Lavandula. Zones vary

TOP Weigela florida. **CENTER** *Golden columbine* (Aquilegia chrysantha). **BOTTOM** *Pincushion flower* (Scabiosa caucasica).

FOR BIRDS AND BUTTERFLIES

Birds and butterflies add special charm to a cottage garden—and with this plan, you'll be enjoying these colorful airborne visitors frequently throughout the growing season (and even beyond). Many of the flowers here offer nectar that will lure butterflies and hummingbirds during the bloom period; others produce seeds to attract seed-eating birds in late summer and fall. All the plants noted in the list below will succeed in Zones 2–9, 14–20, 31–41. To adapt the plan to Zones 21–24 as well, simply replace *Penstemon barbatus* (U in the plan) with *Penstemon × gloxinioides* 'Firebird'.

K. *Sedum* 'Autumn Joy' (3)

L. *Salvia nemorosa* 'Ostfriesland' (3)

M. *Heuchera sanguinea.* Coral bells (9)

N. *Cleome hasslerana.* Spider flower (1)

O. *Dianthus gratianopolitanus.* Cheddar pink (4)

P. *Iberis sempervirens* 'Purity' or 'Snowflake'. Evergreen candytuft (4)

Q. *Antirrhinum majus,* Rocket strain. Snapdragon (6)

R. *Scabiosa atropurpurea,* white-flowered. Pincushion flower (4)

S. *Calendula officinalis.* Pot marigold (6)

T. *Nicotiana,* Nicki strain (10)

U. *Penstemon barbatus* (2) OR *Penstemon × gloxinioides* 'Firebird' (2)*

V. *Cosmos bipinnatus,* Sonata series (4)

W. *Nicotiana,* Domino strain (5)

X. *Lobularia maritima.* Sweet alyssum (8)

* Use the second choice listed if you live in Zones 21–24.

A. *Agastache foeniculum.* Anise hyssop (2)

B. *Alcea rosea.* Hollyhock (6)

C. *Centranthus ruber* 'Albus'. Jupiter's beard (1)

D. *Asclepias tuberosa.* Butterfly weed (3)

E. *Achillea* 'Coronation Gold'. Yarrow (2)

F. *Achillea millefolium,* Summer Pastels strain. Common yarrow (4)

G. *Echinacea purpurea.* Purple cone-flower (3)

H. *Chrysanthemum maximum* 'Alaska'. Shasta daisy (7)

I. *Coreopsis tinctoria.* Annual coreopsis (12)

J. *Liatris spicata.* Gayfeather (1)

LESS-THIRSTY PLANTS

Wherever water is scarce or costly, plants that need less than regular moisture are smart choices. Most of the following flourish with just moderate amounts of water; they don't require constantly moist soil. Particularly drought-tolerant individuals are marked with an asterisk.

Annuals

Calendula officinalis. Zones 1–45, H1

Centaurea cyanus. Zones 1–45, H1, H2

Convolvulus tricolor. Zones 1–45

Coreopsis tinctoria. Zones 1–45, H1, H2

Cosmos bipinnatus. Zones A3, 1–45

Eschscholzia californica. Zones 1–45, H1

Portulaca grandiflora. All zones

Verbena. All zones

Perennials

Achillea. A1–A3, 1–24, 26, 28–45

Agastache. Zones vary

Asclepias tuberosa. Zones 1–45

Aurinia saxatilis. Zones 1–24, 32–43

Centranthus ruber. Zones 2–9, 12–24, 28–43, H1

Echinacea purpurea. Zones A2, A3, 1–24, 26–45

Gypsophila paniculata. Zones A2, A3, 1–10, 14–16, 18–21, 31–45, H1

Lychnis coronaria. Zones 1–9, 14–24, 30, 32, 34–43

Stachys. Zones 1–24, 29–43

Vines

Lonicera. Zones vary

Wisteria. Zones vary

Shrubs

Caryopteris × *clandonensis.* Zones 2b–9, 14–24, 29–41

**Phlomis fruticosa.* Zones 3b–24, 31, warmer 32

Trees

Crataegus. Zones vary

Lagerstroemia indica. Zones 6–10, 12–31, warmer 32, H1, H2

Pyrus calleryana. Zones 2b–9, 14–21, 28, 31–41

Ornamental grasses

**Muhlenbergia.* Zones vary

**Panicum virgatum.* Zones 1–11, 14–23, 28–43

**Pennisetum setaceum.* Zones 8–24, 26, 27, warmer 28, 29, H1, H2

Stipa gigantea. Zones 4–9, 14–24, 29–34, 39

Herbs

**Artemisia* (most). Zones vary

Foeniculum vulgare. Zones 2b–11, 14–24, 29–41, H1, H2

Lavandula. Zones vary

Nepeta. Zones 1–24, 30, 32–43

**Origanum.* Zones vary

**Santolina chamaecyparissus.* Zones 2–24, 27, 29, 30, 32–35, 39, H1, H2

Teucrium chamaedrys. Zones 2–24, 28–41

Thymus. Zones vary

* Especially drought-tolerant choice

TOP *Catmint* (Nepeta sibirica). **CENTER** *Yarrow* (Achillea 'Moonshine'). **BOTTOM** *Lamb's ears* (Stachys byzantina).

A LESS-THIRSTY PLANTING

When the water supply is unlimited, there's no trick to having a lush-looking garden. But not all regions are blessed with abundant water. And even where it is plentiful, it must be applied often during hot summer weather to keep things looking good. If constraints on available water or available time make frequent watering impractical, build your garden with plants that get by with just moderate moisture during the growing season—like this grouping, suited to Zones 3–10, 14–24, 32–34, 39. Gardeners in Zones 2b, 30, 35–38, 40, and 41 can achieve the same general look by replacing the Oriental fountain grass (J in the plan) with tufted fescue *(Festuca amethystina)* and the lavender (L) with blue mist *(Caryopteris ×
clandonensis).*

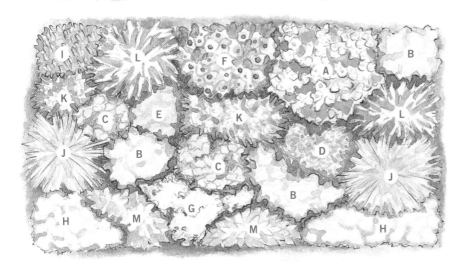

F. *Echinacea purpurea.* Purple cone-
flower (3)

G. *Verbena × hybrida.* Garden verbena
(5)

H. *Euphorbia polychroma.* Cushion
spurge (5)

I. *Agastache foeniculum.* Anise hyssop
(2)

J. *Pennisetum orientale.* Oriental fountain grass (2) OR *Festuca amethystina.* Tufted fescue (2)*

K. *Nepeta grandiflora.* Catmint (3)

L. *Lavandula angustifolia.* English lavender (2) OR *Caryopteris × clandonensis.* Blue mist (2)*

M. *Stachys byzantina* 'Silver Carpet'.
Lamb's ears. (6)

* Use the second choice listed if you live
in Zones 2b, 30, 35–38, 40, or 41.

A. *Hibiscus syriacus* 'Blue Bird'. Rose of
Sharon (1)

B. *Achillea* 'Moonshine'. Yarrow. (7)

C. *Asclepias tuberosa.* Butterfly weed
(5)

D. *Scabiosa atropurpurea.* Pincushion
flower (5)

E. *Coreopsis tinctoria.* Annual coreopsis
(3)

ROUTINE GARDEN CARE

Three maintenance aids—wheelbarrow, watering can, and trowel—are indispensable helpmates for transport, watering, and planting.

Though cottage gardens look carefree, they still need at least some attention if they are to thrive. Here's a basic maintenance roster.

WATERING

Rare is the garden that prospers on rainfall alone all year long. And even where rainfall is common during the growing season, gardeners must be able to provide water when Nature fails. Overhead watering from sprinklers is effective, but it does have a disadvantage: the water can weigh plants down, causing weaker-stemmed ones to lean or sprawl. A better choice for the cottage garden is a drip irrigation system, which effectively applies water at ground level. Such systems are especially good choices where water is in limited supply, since their emitters deliver water slowly, with the precise rate depending on the current water pressure.

FERTILIZING When you first prepare and plant a bed, the new soil and any amendments you've incorporated before planting should be adequate to ensure a good performance over the course of a year or more. To guarantee continued lavish shows, however, plan on annual applications of fertilizer. Because most cottage garden plants are robust and inherently unfussy, one nutrient boost each year—best delivered just as the grow-ing season gets underway—should get them through a season. The easiest products to use are commercial water-soluble granular fertilizers. Scatter the granules over the soil according to the directions on the package, then water them in (unless a well-timed rainstorm does the job for you).

WEEDING AND MULCHING

Weed seeds need moisture and sunlight to germinate. Once your cottage garden is established, the interlacing plants will effectively prevent weed-seed germination by keeping light from the soil. In the early years, however, you'll have patches of bare earth—and thus, weeds—between plants. To deal with these unwelcome arrivals, spread a generous layer of mulch over the soil. It will keep the seeds in the dark, thus discouraging germination; and any weeds that do manage to sprout will be easy to pull. What's more, mulching helps conserve moisture by keeping the surface of the soil cool.

COPING WITH PESTS AND DISEASES Plant predators are inevitable, but before you take action against them, assess the problem and its severity. A minor amount of pest activity or damage won't do much harm to a healthy garden. But if an insect or disease appears to be getting the upper hand, consider appropriate controls. Always begin with the simplest, safest method: handpicking pests or damaged foliage. If that fails, turn to the least toxic option (consult your Cooperative Extension Office). And remember—prevention in the form of garden cleanup (see below) is your first line of defense against potential trouble.

STAKING Many plants are entirely self-supporting, and some of the more lax growers will be naturally propped up by plants growing closely around them. But particularly tall sorts like hollyhock (*Alcea*) and delphinium may need staking if they're to remain vertical throughout the flowering period.

ANNUAL CLEANUP After the growing season ends each year, it's a good idea to clean up your plantings. Besides improving the garden's appearance, the removal of dead leaves and stems eliminates a potential refuge for insects (and their eggs) and disease spores. Clearing out each season's debris also improves air circulation through the planting during the growing season, thus making conditions less favorable for pests and diseases.

Tidying up after annuals is easy: you simply remove and discard the plants. For perennials that die down completely at year's end, remove the season's dead growth; for those that retain some branch structure, clear out all spent leaves and flowers. Once deciduous shrubs and trees have dropped their leaves, clear them away. Leafy evergreen shrubs and trees, too, drop some leaves throughout the year, and these should be raked out from under the branches.

The best time for your annual cleanup depends on the climate. Where winters are cold and snowy, you can do the job in fall, before the garden disappears—or in early spring, before growth gets underway. In milder regions, late fall to early spring (depending on the weather) is prime time. Where there's essentially no winter (Zones 24, 25, 27, H2), midwinter is usually the time for cleanup, since the garden is least active then.

DIVIDING Perennial plants come back year after year, but they vary in their ability to sustain peak performance. Some, like peony (*Paeonia*), will thrive for the lifetime of the gardener without any intervention. Others, such as columbine (*Aquilegia*), will play themselves out after a number of years and need to be replaced by new plants. Most perennials, however, form ever-expanding clumps that become crowded over time; when the clumps become too dense, performance declines. The solution is to dig up the clump, divide it into individual plants (or into small groups of plants), and replant in rejuvenated soil. For each perennial described in Chapter 4, we note how often division is likely to be needed.

PRUNING Most shrubs and semiwoody perennials need occasional pruning to remain shapely, and some will need at least a modicum of annual attention to remove dead and weak stems. Spring-flowering shrubs are best pruned after bloom has ended, when they're starting to put on new growth that will bear the next year's flowers; summer-flowering types can be pruned in early spring, before growth gets underway. Repeat-flowering roses are best pruned just before growth begins each year—in late winter or early spring, depending on climate. Late winter to early spring also is the best time to cut back semiwoody perennials.

Trees may need some annual pruning in their early years, as they develop a permanent structure. Thereafter, any pruning is usually done as needed (not necessarily every year) to keep the tree well shaped. Fruit trees, however, may need more frequent and specific pruning if you're aiming for a good crop each year. Do any tree pruning in winter (in milder regions) or early spring (in colder areas).

CHAPTER FOUR

A ❧ POTPOURRI OF FAVORITE COTTAGE GARDEN PLANTS

Cottage gardens are eclectic and free spirited by nature: the composition varies with the whim of the gardener. Anything goes, as long as it satisfies some personal idea of beauty and flourishes in the local climate. Nonetheless, certain plants are longtime favorites for cottage gardens, chosen again and again because they succeed so beautifully in creating the classic relaxed, free-blooming effect. In this chapter, you'll meet these tried and true individuals and see just what has made them so popular for so long.

This luxuriant planting shows off a wide selection of cottage garden favorites, from flowering annuals and perennials to shrubs, vines, and trees. In a twist on tradition, the entry walk nearly parallels the house as it leads through the garden toward the front door.

ANNUALS

Annuals complete their life cycle within a single growing season: the seed germinates and the plant grows, flowers, sets seed, and dies. Many gardeners, however, interrupt this natural cycle by removing spent blossoms—thus encouraging continued flowering by preventing seed formation. But others prefer to let their annuals set and scatter seed, ensuring a crop of new plants for the following year (plants that seed themselves particularly successfully are described as "self-sowers"). Cool-season annuals grow and flower during spring (and cool summers), then decline when the weather heats up. Warm-season types are at their prime in summer and survive until frosts lay them low; in the mildest regions, some may even live into a second year.

In the home garden, a number of annuals can easily be grown from seed, while others do better if set out as young plants. The favorites described in this section are self-supporting; for vining annuals, turn to page 70.

Antirrhinum majus

Calendula officinalis

Centaurea cyanus

ANTIRRHINUM majus

SNAPDRAGON

Zones A3, 1–45. Full sun; regular water. Cool season.

From spring into early summer, snapdragons offer tapered, vertical flower spikes packed with blossoms in a rainbow of colors. Plants are narrow, upright growers with narrow leaves. Many named strains are sold, from dwarf kinds under a foot tall to the more traditional sorts that grow as large as 3 feet high and 2 feet wide. Flower types vary as well, including not only the familiar "snapping" kind (squeeze the flower lightly and it opens its "jaws"), but also double sorts and those with bell-shaped and azalealike blooms. Where winters are mild, set out plants in fall; in colder regions, plant in spring.

CALENDULA officinalis

CALENDULA, POT MARIGOLD

Zones 1–45, H1. Full sun; moderate water. Cool season. Self-sower.

Formerly grown for the kitchen (hence the common name "pot marigold"), this bright-blossomed plant is now treasured simply for the beauty it brings to the cool-season garden. Daisy flowers up to 4 inches across may be single, semidouble, or double; colors include orange, yellow, cream, and white. The plant is bushy to spreading, with slightly sticky leaves; depending on the strain, size varies from 1 to $2\frac{1}{2}$ feet high, 1 to $1\frac{1}{2}$ feet wide. In mild-winter areas, set out young plants in fall; they'll bloom from winter until hot weather strikes. In colder regions, set out as soon as soil is workable for a long spring-into-summer show.

CENTAUREA cyanus

CORNFLOWER, BACHELOR'S BUTTON

Zones 1–45, H1, H2. Full sun; moderate water. Cool season.

Wispy cornflower is a longtime favorite for the spring and early summer garden, cherished for its distinctive thistlelike, $1\frac{1}{2}$-inch flowers. Medium blue is the traditional color, but you'll also find strains with blossoms in white, purple, wine red, and pink. Several plants grouped together give the best color impact, but individual specimens popping up here and there among other flowers truly capture the cottage garden spirit. Plants are upright growers to 1½ feet tall and less than a foot wide.

Cornflower is best grown from seed (young plants don't transplant easily). Sow directly in the garden—in fall in mild-winter regions, near the last-frost date in colder regions. If the last flowers of the season are left to go to seed, some volunteer seedlings will appear the next year.

CLEOME hasslerana (C. spinosa)
SPIDER FLOWER

Zones 1—45. Full sun; moderate to regular water. Warm season. Self-sower.

Spider flower grows fast: a slender seedling quickly bulks up to a shrublike, thickly foliaged mass to 5 feet tall and nearly as wide. In summer and fall, stems terminate in large, loose flower clusters; each blossom has extremely long, protruding, spidery-looking stamens, hence the common name. Long, narrow, decorative seedpods follow the flowers. In most selections, the stems are armed with short spines. Pink and white are the usual colors, but named varieties come in other hues, including purple, rose, and cherry pink. Sow seeds directly in the garden after all danger of frost is past; or set out nursery plants at that time.

CONSOLIDA ajacis (C. ambigua)
LARKSPUR, ANNUAL DELPHINIUM

Zones 1—45. Full sun; regular water. Cool season. Self-sower.

Larkspur truly is the annual equivalent of perennial delphini-

um—with the bonus of being easier to grow over a wider climatic range. Depending on the strain, the plant reaches 1 to 4 feet high and up to 1 foot wide, producing slender spikes of spurred, 1- to 1½-inch-wide flowers above feathery-looking, finely cut foliage. Most popular are the double-flowered sorts, available in white, blue, lavender, purple, pink, salmon, and even some bicolors.

Larkspur thrives in cool weather, dying out in the heat of summer. For best results, sow seeds outdoors in fall—unless you're planting in heavy clay soil, in which case it's best to sow in spring, about 2 weeks before the last-frost date.

COREOPSIS tinctoria
ANNUAL COREOPSIS, CALLIOPSIS

Zones 1—45, H1, H2. Full sun; little to moderate water. Warm season. Self-sower.

This native North American daisy really needs no care at all! A slender, upright plant with narrow, lacy-looking leaves, it sends up needle-thin stems to 1½ to 3 feet, each bearing a single 2-inch blossom. The basic color is brassy yellow, but named selections include variations with maroon centers and with petals striped, banded, or tipped in combinations of yellow and purplish brown.

Sow seeds directly in the garden after the danger of frost is past; you'll have blossoms from summer into fall.

Cleome hasslerana

Consolida ajacis

Coreopsis tinctoria

Cosmos bipinnatus

Eschscholzia californica

Gomphrena globosa

COSMOS bipinnatus

COSMOS

Zones A3, 1–45. Full sun; moderate water. Warm season. Self-sower.

The basic species is an upright plant to 6 feet tall and 2½ feet wide, outfitted in extremely finely cut, almost threadlike foliage. It blooms from summer into fall, bearing broad-petaled, 3- to 4-inch daisies in white, pink shades, red, purple, and lavender. Plant breeders have had a field day with cosmos, creating strains in heights ranging from 1½ to 6 feet; some have semidouble flowers, and the Seashells strain has rolled petals that look like macaroni tubes.

Sow seeds directly in the garden after the danger of frost is past; or set out started young plants then.

ESCHSCHOLZIA californica

CALIFORNIA POPPY

Zones 1–45, H1. Full sun; little to moderate water. Cool season. Self-sower.

From late winter or early spring (depending on climate) until hot weather settles in, California poppy puts on a nonstop show of silky-petaled blossoms. From a clump of filigreelike gray-green leaves, slender stems rise 1 to 2 feet, each carrying a chalice-shaped, 2-inch flower. The typical colors are orange and orange-centered yellow, but cream to white variants also occur naturally—and seed strains offer these and many other colors, including pink, wine red, purple, apricot, orange red, and yellow (some strains have semidouble to double flowers).

Sow seeds directly in the garden—in fall where winters are mild, in early spring in colder areas. In mild-winter regions, let plants self-sow (seeds will germinate in fall); where winters are cold, collect seeds for sowing the next spring.

GOMPHRENA globosa

GLOBE AMARANTH

Zones 1–45, H1, H2. Full sun or partial shade; moderate water. Warm season.

From summer into fall, masses of papery, ½-inch flower heads resembling clover blossoms come on an upright to spreading plant to 2 feet tall. Colors include lavender, purple, red, pink, and white; among named selections, you'll find separate colors as well as dwarf types reaching just 10 inches high. Like cornflower (*Centaurea*), this plant is individually insubstantial and makes the greatest color impact if set out in groups, but it also looks delightful growing among other annuals and perennials.

Sow seeds or set out young nursery plants directly in the garden after all danger of frost is past. In the mildest regions, the plants may live over the winter to bloom a second year. Globe amaranth will self-sow when the conditions are right, giving you a modest crop of volunteer seedlings.

LOBULARIA maritima

SWEET ALYSSUM

All zones. Full sun; regular water.
Cool and warm season. Self-sower.
Fragrant.

If it weren't so pretty, you'd call it a weed! The plant is a low, bushy mound of tiny leaves, but during bloom time, you can hardly see the foliage: it's covered in dome-shaped clusters of small, honey-scented flowers. Colors include white, pink, lavender, and purple; named selections come in separate as well as mixed colors. Among your choices are pink 'Pink Heather' and 'Rosie O'Day', violet 'Oriental Night' and 'Violet Queen', and the mixed-color 'Pastel Carpet'. Bloom runs from spring through fall (and even into winter, in the mildest regions).

Depending on the selection, sweet alyssum ranges from 2 to 12 inches tall, 8 to 12 inches across. It begins to look a bit sparse and ragged toward the end of the year's long bloom season; to keep it more compact, shear it back by about half after the first flush of flowers.

Sow seeds directly in the garden or set out young plants—in fall in mild-winter locales, a few weeks after the last frost where winters are cold. After an initial planting, you can count on an annual crop of volunteers to keep things going. (Note that colored selections will revert to white or pale lavender after several volunteer generations.)

MYOSOTIS sylvatica

FORGET-ME-NOT

Zones A1–A3, 1–24, 32–45.
Partial shade; regular to ample
water. Cool season. Self-sower.

Forget-me-not is well known (and well loved) for its color—a pure, sparkling blue. From early spring (or even midwinter, in mild climates) until hot weather arrives, open sprays of $1/4$-inch, yellow-eyed flowers adorn a bushy plant to 1 foot high, about 2 feet wide. The tongue-shaped, hairy leaves are bright green. Named forget-me-not selections include 'Rosylva', with pink flowers; the Victoria series, with blooms in blue, pink, and white; and several lower, more compact growers.

In mild-winter regions, sow seeds directly in the garden in fall; in colder areas, sow several weeks before the last-frost date. After you've sown seeds once, volunteer seedlings can keep you in plants for years to come.

NICOTIANA

All zones. Full sun, except as noted;
regular water. Warm season.
Fragrant.

No garden of scented plants would be complete without nicotiana. In mid- to late spring or summer, loose clusters of flowers are carried on leafy, upright stems that rise from clumps of large, oval leaves; each blossom is a narrow tube that flares into a star shape about 2 inches across. Both foliage and stems are slightly sticky. Most of the plants sold

Lobularia maritima

Myosotis sylvatica

Nicotiana, **Nicki strain**

today are hybrids (sometimes listed as *N. × sanderae*) ranging from 1 to 3½ feet tall; flower colors include green, white, cream, pink, red, and purple. For guaranteed powerful fragrance, look for white-blossomed, night-blooming 'Grandiflora' or the mixed-color Heavenscent series, both at the upper end of the height range.

Set out started plants after the last-frost date. Give full sun except in hot-summer regions, where plants appreciate dappled sun or light afternoon shade.

NIGELLA damascena

LOVE-IN-A-MIST

All zones. Full sun or partial shade; regular water. Cool season. Self-sower.

An essential for the cottage garden, this old-fashioned spring bloomer is a wispy, narrow, 2-foot-tall plant with filigreelike foliage and fringe-petaled, 1- to 1½-inch-wide blossoms backed by an Elizabethan ruff of thread-like segments. Colors include white, blue, violet, and pink; named strains are sold in individual as well as mixed colors. After the flowers fade, decorative horned, papery seed capsules put on another display.

Sow seeds directly in the garden—in autumn where winters are mild, 2 to 3 weeks before the last-frost date in colder regions. After the first year, self-sowing will keep love-in-a-mist in your garden—if you let the capsules mature, they'll scat-

Nigella damascena

Papaver rhoeas

ter seeds for crops of volunteers that will spring up here and there, to charming effect.

PAPAVER

POPPY

Zones vary. Full sun; moderate to regular water. Cool season. Self-sowers.

Though poppy plants vary in appearance and size, all present their flowers the same way. A slender, often wire-thin stem rises upward, then bends to form a "gooseneck" that holds at its tip a single fat, oval bud. When the bud is ready to open, the stem straightens and a single or double bloom emerges. Single blossoms are bowl shaped, often centered with a contrasting color, while double ones look like pom-poms—but both kinds have silky, crinkled or creased petals. After the petals fall, decorative seed capsules resembling flat-topped spheres appear; if left to ripen, they'll provide seeds for next year's plants.

Flanders field or Shirley poppy, *P. rhoeas,* grows in Zones A1–A3, 1–24, 26, 28–45. This is the single bright red poppy of European grain fields. It's still available in that basic form, but more modern versions are also sold, including single and double, 2- to 3-inch-wide flowers in a striking color array—white, soft blue, lilac, pink, salmon, red, orange, and bicolor combinations. Clothed in deeply cut pale green leaves, the plants are slender, branching, upright growers that reach 2 to 3 feet high and about 1 foot wide.

Performance is best in cooler weather. Where winters are mild, sow seeds outdoors in fall for bloom as early in spring as possible. In colder regions, sow up to 1 month before the last-frost date for the best shot at flowers before the weather heats up.

Breadbox or opium poppy, *P. somniferum,* succeeds in all zones. The plant grows upright to 4 feet tall and 1 foot wide, with striking broad, somewhat jagged-edged gray-green leaves ascending the stems. Flowers are up to 5 inches across; the basic form has single lilac-pink blooms, but a double-flowered version is also sold, as are double strains in white, bright red, salmon pink, plum purple, and blackish maroon. This poppy is the source of culinary poppy seed. For planting times, see *P. rhoeas* (above).

PORTULACA grandiflora
ROSE MOSS
All zones. Full sun; moderate water. Warm season. Self-sower.

Charming planted along a pathway, rose moss is a low, spreading plant that covers itself with bright, silky blossoms during the worst of summer's heat. Resembling inch-wide roses, the flowers may be single, semidouble, or double; they typically open in the morning and close in midafternoon, though some strains remain open until late in the day. Colors include cream, yellow, orange, red, pink, purple, and

multicolors. Plants reach about 6 inches high and 1 foot wide, with succulent reddish stems clothed in fleshy, inch-long, almost cylindrical leaves.

Sow seeds directly in the garden after all danger of frost is past; or set out young plants then. Volunteer seedlings will furnish plants in subsequent years, though the color variety will eventually decrease.

RESEDA odorata
MIGNONETTE
All zones. Full sun, except as noted; regular water. Cool season. Fragrant.

No one would call mignonette beautiful: the spikes of tiny greenish gold flowers aren't showy, and the 1- to $1\frac{1}{2}$-foot-high plants are a bit sprawling. But once you experience the fragrance, you'll understand why gardeners have been growing mignonette for generations, tucking it in among showier specimens just for the benefit of its spicy-sweet scent.

Sow seeds directly in the garden—in fall or winter where winters are relatively mild, in early spring in colder areas. Give full sun except in hot-summer regions, where a lightly shaded location is better.

SALVIA viridis (S. horminum)
ANNUAL CLARY
All zones. Full sun; regular water. Warm season.

Reaching 2 feet high and 1 foot wide, this fast-growing, bushy but

Portulaca grandiflora

Reseda odorata

Salvia viridis, **Bouquet Mix**

Annuals | **47**

Scabiosa atropurpurea

Tropaeolum majus, Alaska strain

Verbena × hybrida 'Quartz Burgundy'

upright plant comes into bloom in early summer. Small, creamy to pinkish flowers are borne in upright spikes, but the blossoms themselves are not that striking: it's the decorative, dark-veined, 1½-inch bracts beneath each flower that put on the display. Bracts come in white, pink, or violet and remain attractive even after they've dried.

Sow seeds directly in the garden as soon as the danger of frost is past; or set out started young plants then.

SCABIOSA atropurpurea
PINCUSHION FLOWER, MOURNING BRIDE
Zones 1–45, H1, H2. Full sun; moderate to regular water. Warm season. Fragrant.

Graceful pincushion flower is the embodiment of old-style charm. Clumps of coarsely toothed leaves produce wandlike stems to 3 feet tall, each topped by a nosegaylike, 2- to 3-inch-wide cluster of small, sweetly fragrant flowers; the blossoms have prominent stamens, reminiscent of pins in a pincushion. Colors include white, lavender, violet, pink, dark red, and nearly black; you can buy strains in mixed as well as individual colors, and there are also varieties reaching just 1½ to 2½ feet high. Bloom starts in early to midsummer and continues until autumn frost.

Sow seeds directly in the garden after the danger of frost is past; or set out started young plants then.

TROPAEOLUM majus
NASTURTIUM
All zones. Full sun or light shade; regular water. Cool season. Self-sower.

Here are bushy versions of the familiar vining nasturtiums described on page 71. The same near-circular leaves and spurred, trumpet-shaped flowers in cream, maroon, and bright shades of orange, red, and yellow come on plants that vary in height from just 6 inches to about 2 feet, depending on the selection. The Alaska strain has leaves splotched and marbled in white.

Planting times are the same as for vining kinds; see page 71.

VERBENA
All zones. Full sun; moderate water. Warm season.

For brilliant pathway color, nothing beats verbenas. Flowering virtually throughout the growing season, these spreading plants pump out an unending supply of flat-topped flower heads in a wide range of colors—some soft, some bright. Plants may live for several years in mild-winter zones, but even there most gardeners treat them as annuals.

Garden verbena, *V. × hybrida (V. × hortensis),* is a hybrid group of dense-foliaged plants up to a foot high and 3 feet across, covered at bloom time in 3-inch blossom clusters. You'll find flowers in white, blue, purple, pink, or red; the colored forms usually have a white central eye. Strains are available in individual as well as mixed colors. Lower-growing *V. peruviana (V. chamaedrifolia)* makes a ground-hugging foliage mat that spreads to 3 feet or more; it bears white-centered scarlet flowers. Named selections are a bit taller (to about 6 inches high) and come in pink shades, red, purple, and white.

For both verbenas, set out young plants just after the last-frost date.

VIOLA

Thanks to their simple country charm, pansies, violas, and Johnny jump-ups are cottage garden classics. All are bushy to sprawling plants with five-petaled, flat-faced flowers carried individually at the tips of slender stems. Bloom begins in winter (in the mildest regions) or spring and continues until hot weather arrives; in cool-summer regions, plants may flower throughout summer.

Johnny jump-up, *V. tricolor,* grows in all zones. It reaches about 1 foot high and wide and is the smallest in leaf and flower—the purple-and-yellow or blue-and-yellow blooms are no more than $^3/_4$ inch across. Blossoms come in great profusion, though, and the plant self-sows freely.

Viola or tufted pansy, *V. cornuta,* succeeds in Zones A2, A3, 1–24, 29–45. Reaching about 8 inches high and wide, it bears 1- to 2-inch flowers in a wide range of colors. You can buy named individual-color selections; bicolor combinations are also sold, including some with "whisker pattern" veins on the petals.

Pansy, *V. × wittrockiana,* flourishes in all zones. It's the show-off of the viola trio, bearing flowers to 4 inches across that come in a seemingly endless variety of colors, including orange, red, mahogany, brown, near-black, purple, lavender, pink, blue, white, cream, and yellow. You can find solid colors, but multi- and bicolors are much more common; the lower three petals of each flower are often marked with a dark, velvety blotch. Countless named strains and selections are available. Plants can reach about 1 foot high and wide.

Johnny jump-ups, violas, and pansies all grow in full sun or partial shade; where summers are hot, a partially shaded location will help prolong bloom. For pansies and violas in particular, remove spent flowers to keep blooms coming. In cool regions, cut back lightly in summer to encourage a last good flowering in late summer to early fall.

For all three plants, winter temperatures determine planting time. In mild-winter regions, set out young plants in fall. Where winters are cold, sow seed indoors 10 to 12 weeks before the last-frost date; then set out the resulting seedlings (or purchased nursery plants) in early spring for flowers by early summer.

Viola tricolor

Viola × wittrockiana 'Joker Poker Face'

Think of biennials as slow annuals. You plant seeds in the spring or summer of one year; the seeds germinate and grow into husky plants by fall, then wait until the next year to flower. (Biennials can also be started from nursery plants; these are typically set out in late summer to early fall for bloom the following spring or summer.) Plants inclined to self-sow will produce a crop of seedlings to keep replacements coming along.

Alcea rosea

Campanula medium 'Calycanthema'

ALCEA rosea (Althaea rosea)

HOLLYHOCK

Zones 1–45. Full sun, except as noted; regular water. Self-sower.

Classics of the cottage garden, hollyhocks are quintessential vertical accents. Large, nearly round leaves form a mounding clump to 3 feet wide; tall stems rise from the foliage in summer, plastered with saucer-shaped, 3- to 6-inch blossoms in a wide range of colors. Numerous named strains are available, varying in stalk height from 2½ to 8 feet; some kinds have double blooms that look like fluffy powderpuffs.

By nature, these plants are biennial, but many modern strains live a bit longer, functioning as short-lived perennials. And so-called annual strains bloom the first year from seed (where winters are mild, sow in early spring; in colder climates, start indoors and set out after the danger of frost is past). Give full sun except in the hottest regions, where plants do better in partial shade.

CAMPANULA medium

CANTERBURY BELLS

Zones 1–9, 14-24, 31–45. Full sun, except as noted; regular water.

Wherever they'll grow easily, Canterbury bells are a must-have for any cottage garden in the classic style. Rising from clumps of narrow leaves, the 2- to 3-foot-tall, leafy stems bear spikes of upward-facing bells to 2 inches across. Lavender and blue are the classic colors, but white, violet, and pink forms are also available. The selection 'Calycanthema' features a circular petal-like ruff behind the bell, giving the blossom a cup-and-saucer appearance.

Annual strains of Canterbury bells exist, but they're short plants—under 1½ feet tall—that lack the presence of the biennial forms. To grow biennials, sow seeds or set out started plants in late spring or early summer for bloom the following spring. Give full sun except in hot-summer areas, where partial shade is better.

DIANTHUS barbatus

SWEET WILLIAM

Zones A2, A3, 1–24, 30–45. Full sun; moderate to regular water. Self-sower. Fragrant.

Immediately recognizable as a carnation relative, this bushy, narrow-leafed plant grows to 20 inches tall and about a foot wide, offering dense clusters of spicy-scented, circular, ½-inch flowers with fringed petal margins. The basic colors are white, pink, and red; most varieties feature bicolor blooms, usually with a lighter central eye and/or petal edging.

Numerous named strains are sold, including shorter-growing types and even a few that will bloom the first year from seed sown in early spring. For the standard biennial sorts of sweet William, however, sow seeds in late spring for flowers the following spring.

DIGITALIS purpurea
FOXGLOVE
Zones A2, A3, 1–24, 31–41. Light shade, except as noted; regular water. Self-sower.

Though perennial foxgloves exist, the most familiar kind is this biennial favorite. In its first year, the plant forms a clump of large, tongue-shaped leaves. The next spring, a sturdy stem rises from the clump's center to about 6 feet, bedecked with pendent, thimble-shaped, 2- to 3-inch-long flowers in cream, white, rosy purple, or pink—typically spotted heavily with purple on the inside ('Alba' has unspotted blooms). Named strains include Excelsior, with outward-facing blossoms, and some shorter sorts—such as 3-foot Foxy, which blooms in just 5 months from seed and can serve as an annual.

For traditional biennial foxgloves, sow seeds outdoors in late spring or summer for bloom the following spring. Choose a spot in light shade; in cool-summer climates, plants will also do well in full sun.

ERYSIMUM
WALLFLOWER
Zones vary. Full sun or light shade; water needs vary. Fragrant.

Where climate permits, no traditional cottage garden is complete without wallflowers. Borne in clusters strewn over narrow-leafed plants, the four-petaled, ¹/₂-inch flowers (though not impressive individually) make a striking color statement.

English wallflower, *E. cheiri (Cheiranthus cheiri),* grows in Zones 4–6, 14–17, 22, 23, 32, 34. It's a branching, woody-based plant that can reach 2¹/₂ feet high and 1¹/₂ feet wide, producing broad clusters of sweet-scented blossoms in cream, yellow, orange, red, warm pink shades, mauve, maroon, and brown. Double-flowered strains are also available. Bloom begins in spring and ceases with the onset of really warm weather; where summers are very cool, though, you'll get flowers right through the summer (and even into autumn). Give this species regular water.

Siberian wallflower, *E. × allionii,* succeeds in Zones A3, 1–9, 14–24, 32–43. Growing to 1¹/₂ feet high and about 2 feet wide, it offers a springtime display of scented yellow or orange blossoms. It does best with moderate watering.

For either species, you can set out young plants or sow seeds—in fall in mild-winter regions, in early spring where winters are cold.

Dianthus barbatus 'Newport Pink'

Digitalis purpurea, Foxy strain

Erysimum × allionii 'Orange Bedder'

Perennials are those obliging nonwoody plants that return year after year, gracing the garden with their flowers and foliage. They vary enormously, from low-growing sorts that hug the ground to relative giants with the bulk of shrubs. Some live for several years, then decline and need replacement; others increase to form crowded clumps that require periodic digging and separating to regain their original vigor. And a smaller number—like butterfly weed (Asclepias) and peony (Paeonia)—are long-lived, noninvasive plants that flourish for years from an initial planting, never needing replacement or division.

Achillea millefolium

Agastache foeniculum

ACHILLEA

YARROW

Zones A1–A3, 1–24, 26, 28–45. Full sun; little to moderate water.

Though their sizes and shapes vary, most yarrows have two characteristics in common: finely divided, almost fernlike foliage and tiny, daisylike flowers densely packed into flat-topped or somewhat rounded heads. Spreading, ground-hugging types—good for pathway planting—include Greek yarrow (*A. ageratifolia,* also known as *A. serbica*) and silvery yarrow (*A. clavennae*), both with silver gray foliage and small, flat clusters of white flowers on stems to 10 inches. Woolly yarrow, *A. tomentosa,* is another low spreader with stems to 10 inches; it has gray-green leaves and yellow blossoms.

Two hybrids—*A.* × *taygetea* (to 1½ feet) and *A.* 'Moonshine' (to 2 feet)—are gray-green, bushy plants with yellow blossom clusters around 2 inches across. Common yarrow, *A. millefolium,* is a rounded, billowy plant available in numerous selections and strains that vary from 2 to 4 feet high and wide. Colors include red, pink, yellow, white, and bicolor combinations.

Tallest of the popular yarrows is fernleaf yarrow, *A. filipendulina,* which forms an upright clump to 5 feet tall, 3 feet wide. Its deep yellow selection 'Gold Plate' has 6-inch flower heads; the hybrid 'Coronation Gold' is shorter (to 3 feet), with flower heads to about 4 inches. When clumps of any yarrow become crowded, divide them in spring.

AGASTACHE

GIANT HYSSOP

Zones vary. Full sun or partial shade; moderate water.

As the common name implies, these vigorous, summer-blooming plants do indeed look like oversize versions of hyssop *(Hyssopus),* featuring the same tidy, bushy growth bursting with slender spikes of small flowers. Two species are adapted to a range of climates and can tolerate cold, damp winters; both have licorice-scented foliage. The hardier of the two is anise hyssop, *A. foeniculum* (Zones A3, 1–24, 28–41), a narrow, densely foliaged 3-footer bearing spikes of lilac-blue flowers. The leaves can be infused in water to make a pleasant tea.

Korean hummingbird mint, *A. rugosa* (Zones 4–24, 28–33), is another narrow plant, reaching 5 to 6 feet high. It has purplish blue blossoms and leaves that are larger and more broadly oval than those of *A. foeniculum.*

A number of other species hail from the Southwest and thrive with heat, dryness, and mild winters. These plants and their hybrids offer flowers not only in cool colors but also in flashy pink, orange, and red shades. They're excellent for the West and Southwest.

For any agastache, divide crowded clumps in spring.

AQUILEGIA
COLUMBINE

Zones vary. Full sun or light shade; regular water. Self-sowers.

Showy, graceful, and delicate looking, columbines are a traditional favorite for the spring garden. The plants resemble a gray-green maidenhair fern—until, that is, they send up stems bearing sprays of the unmistakable columbine blossoms: a loose "cup" of petals sitting on a starlike "saucer" that is typically backed with five backward-projecting spurs. Ranging from $1^1/2$ to 3 inches wide, the flowers may be erect or nodding, in blue, purple, white, pink, red, yellow, orange, or various bicolor combinations.

Short columbines (1 to $2^1/2$ feet high) include red-and-yellow *A. canadensis; A. flabellata,* with lilac-blue or creamy white blooms; and *A. vulgaris,* in blue, violet, and white. All three succeed in Zones A2, A3, 1–9, 14–24, and 32–45; *A. canadensis* also thrives in Zones A1, 10, 30, and 31, and *A. vulgaris* in Zone 10.

Taller species include 3-foot-high Rocky Mountain columbine, *A. caerulea* (Zones A1–A3, 1–11, 14–24, 32–45), with blue flowers, and 4-foot golden columbine, *A. chrysantha* (Zones 1–11, 14–24, 31–45), in pure yellow.

Hybrid strains, successful in Zones A2, A3, 1–10, 14–24, 32–45, are the columbines most widely sold in nurseries. The Music strain, to $1^1/2$ feet, is at the lower end of the height range; McKana Giants and double-flowered Spring Song grow to 3 feet.

Most columbines are not long-lived plants. Plan on replacing them every 3 or 4 years.

ASCLEPIAS tuberosa
BUTTERFLY WEED

Zones 1–45. Full sun; little to moderate water.

Blooming in appropriately sunny colors, butterfly weed is indeed a butterfly magnet. Each spring, new stems rise from a dormant root, forming a clump 2 to 3 feet tall and up to a foot across. In summer, flattened clusters of starlike blossoms appear at the stem tips. Orange is the typical color, but the Gay Butterflies strain offers a mix of individuals in red, orange, pink, yellow, and bicolors, while 'Hello Yellow' is a guaranteed yellow.

In some regions, butterfly weed is a favorite food of monarch butterfly caterpillars, which can devour the clumps almost to the ground (they grow back fast). The plant is long lived and never needs division.

Aquilegia canadensis

Asclepias tuberosa, Gay Butterflies strain

Aster × frikartii 'Wonder of Staffa'

Aurinia saxatilis

Campanula persicifolia

ASTER

Zones vary. Full sun; regular water.

With one exception, these daisies come into flower in late summer, when most other perennials are folding their tents for the year. Typical colors are in the blue-lavender-purple range—especially welcome in the August and September heat.

A. *laevis* bears deep blue, 1-inch flowers on plants to 3½ feet high and 1½ feet wide; it succeeds in Zones 1–10, 14–24, 31–45. The hybrid A. × *frikartii* grows in Zones 2b–24, 31–43; unlike most other asters, it begins bloom in early summer and continues into fall (and can flower nearly throughout the growing season in mild-winter zones). 'Mönch' and 'Wonder of Staffa' are the generally available selections; both of these grow as large as 3 feet high and wide and bear 2- to 3-inch-wide blue-lavender blossoms.

Old-fashioned favorites New England aster (A. *novae-angliae*) and New York aster or Michael-mas daisy (A. *novi-belgii*) grow in Zones 1–24, 31–42. Both are vigorous plants reaching 4 to 5 feet tall and nearly as wide, sending up a multitude of stems that are crowned at bloom time by airy sprays of 2-inch violet-blue flowers. Each has named selections offering shorter plants and a wider color range, including white, pink, and wine red as well as blue and violet.

For all of the above asters, divide crowded clumps in spring.

AURINIA saxatilis (Alyssum saxatile)

BASKET-OF-GOLD
Zones 1–24, 32–43. Full sun; moderate water. Self-sower.

Nothing is better for softening the edges of a pathway than sunny basket-of-gold. The plant forms a foot-tall, 1½-foot-wide mound of narrow gray-green leaves, covered in spring by inch-wide clusters of small, brilliant yellow flowers. Among available selections, you'll find 'Dudley Neville Variegated', with apricot-yellow blossoms and white-edged leaves, and several with pale yellow blooms.

Basket-of-gold declines quickly in regions where summers are hot and humid. Where it's longer lived, you can divide crowded clumps in fall when you need to rejuvenate a planting.

CAMPANULA

BELLFLOWER, CAMPANULA
Zones vary. Full sun, except as noted; moderate to regular water.

Bell-shaped or starlike flowers in violet, blue, white, and cool pink are typical of the many campanulas. The biennial species C. *medium* (see page 50) is a classic for cottage gardens, and the following perennial sorts are just as charming and appropriate. Among these, your choices fall into two groups. One comprises spreading types with flowers typically scattered over the foliage surface; the other includes plants with upright stems bearing spires or clusters of flowers. In most kinds, the blossoms are about 1 inch in diameter.

The two popular spreading types bloom from spring into summer. Dalmatian bellflower, *C. portenschlagiana* (Zones 2–9, 14–24, 31–41), forms a low (4- to 6-inch-high) mound thickly sprinkled with bell-like violet flowers. Serbian bellflower, *C. poscharskyana* (Zones 1–9, 14–24, 31–45), reaches 8 inches tall and spreads widely by rooting runners; its starlike flowers are light blue or white.

Upright campanulas send up leafy flowering stems from low foliage clumps. *C. glomerata* (Zones A1, A2, 1–10, 14–24, 31–45), reaching 1½ to 2 feet tall, is a spring-through-summer bloomer bearing dense clusters of upward- to outward-facing violet bells; named selections come in white as well as different shades of violet. Slender, graceful peach-leafed bluebell, *C. persicifolia* (Zones 1–9, 14–24, 31–45), offers loose spires of outward-facing, bell-shaped summer flowers in blue, white, or pink on stems to 3 feet high. Taller still is summer-blooming *C. lactiflora* (Zones 1–9, 14–24, 31–34, 39), which reaches 3 to 5 feet. Its flowers are nearly starlike, carried in large, conical clusters; colors range from violet to pale blue, white, and pink. Named selections are available.

Give all these campanulas full sun except in warm-summer areas, where they need partial shade. Divide crowded clumps in early spring.

CENTRANTHUS ruber

JUPITER'S BEARD, RED VALERIAN

Zones 2–9, 12–24, 28–43, H1. Full sun or light shade; little to moderate water. Self-sower.

If ever there was a trouble-free plant, Jupiter's beard is it! Tight, bushy clumps of lance-shaped, slightly fleshy leaves send up leafy, upright stems to 3 feet tall. From midspring into summer, the stems are topped by elongated, fluffy clusters of tiny flowers in dusty pink, carmine red, or white. Cut back the spent flower stems to get another wave of bloom later in the summer. When clumps become crowded, divide them in spring.

CHRYSANTHEMUM

Zones vary. Full sun; regular water. C. parthenium is a self-sower.

In addition to the familiar, fluffy autumn-blooming mums, you'll find a number of charming chrysanthemums with simple daisy flowers. Among these are two cottage garden staples.

Feverfew, *C. parthenium (Tanacetum parthenium),* grows in Zones 2–24, 28–45; once planted, it will perpetuate itself with volunteer seedlings. Clumps of feathery bright green leaves with a peppery scent stretch upward to 2 feet or taller in late spring and summer, as stems elongate to bear clusters of inch-wide white daisies. 'Aureum', with chartreuse leaves, is widely available; also sold are shorter variants and double-flowered kinds.

continued on page 56

Centranthus ruber

Chrysanthemum parthenium

Chrysanthemum maximum

Delphinium elatum **hybrid**

Dianthus plumarius **'Cyclops'**

Showy Shasta daisy, *C. maximum (C. × superbum, Leucanthemum maximum, L. × superbum),* grows in Zones A1–A3, 1–24, northern 26, 28–43, H1. Throughout the summer, clumps of toothed, linear leaves send up leafy flower stems, each topped by one to several sizable white daisies. The classic original type bears yellow-centered single blossoms to 4 inches across on 2- to 4-foot stems; numerous named selections offer single, semidouble, and fully double blooms on plants ranging in height from 15 inches to 4 feet.

Both *C. parthenium* and *C. maximum* should be divided when clumps become crowded—*C. parthenium* in spring, *C. maximum* in fall (where winters are mild) or early spring.

DELPHINIUM

Zones A1–A3, 1–10, 14–24, 32, 34, 36–41. Full sun, except as noted; regular water.

No classic English cottage garden is complete without delphiniums' stately blue spires. The 5- to 8-foot stems reach skyward, tightly packed with 2- to 3-inch flowers offering a cool accent in pure blue as well as in violet, pink, white, and bicolors. The most widely planted delphiniums are the summer-blooming *D. elatum* hybrids—especially those of the Pacific strain, which includes numerous named selections in specific colors. These delphiniums reach perfection in climates offering cool to mild summers

with a bit of cool humidity. If grown in warmer, drier conditions, they'll need some shade from summer sun.

Hybrid delphiniums tend to be fairly short lived. When they decline, simply replace them with new young plants.

DIANTHUS

PINK

Zones A2, A3, 1–24, 30–45, except as noted. Full sun, except as noted; moderate to regular water. Fragrant.

These plants have been components of cottage gardens for hundreds of years, and no wonder: their charm, abundant bloom, and spicy fragrance make them irresistible. Sizes vary, but all are built along the same lines. The plants are low mats or mounds of very narrow gray-green to green leaves. Slender, slightly leafy flowering stems rise above the foliage, bearing single to double, $1/2$- to 1-inch-wide blossoms with fringed petals; single flowers are flat and circular in outline, while semidouble and double kinds look more like powderpuffs. Colors include white, innumerable pink shades, red, maroon, and various combinations of two or three colors.

Cheddar pink, *D. gratianopolitanus (D. caesius),* forms a ground-hugging mat with spring-into-fall flowers on stems to 10 inches tall. Maiden pink, *D. deltoides,* has the same habit, but its stems can reach 1 foot; it blooms in summer and sometimes again in fall.

Cottage pink, *D. plumarius* (Zones A1–A3, 1–24, 30–45), is a looser, taller plant bearing blossoms from summer into fall on stems to 1½ feet. Its hybrid, *D × allwoodii,* is about the same size but more compact and earlier blooming (from spring into summer).

In hot-summer climates, locate dianthus where they will receive some light afternoon shade. Most perennial kinds begin to decline after several years and will need to be replaced with new plants.

ECHINACEA purpurea
PURPLE CONEFLOWER

Zones A2, A3, 1–24, 26–45. Full sun; moderate water. Self-sower.

Big, brash daisy flowers come throughout summer on these tough-as-nails plants. Carried on 2- to 4-foot stems above clumps of coarse, sandpapery leaves, the blossoms are typically about 4 inches across, with a dark, beehive-shaped center surrounded by rosy purple petals. In wild forms, the petals usually droop—but named selections offer petals that are held horizontally, and you'll also find varieties with white petals around an orange central cone.

In hot-summer regions, plants will grow in light shade as well as in sun. The clumps are long lived; when they eventually decline, replace them with new plants (you can often simply transplant volunteer seedlings into any empty spaces).

EUPHORBIA
SPURGE

Zones vary. Full sun, except as noted; moderate water. Most are self-sowers.

The spurges are attention getters! Plants and flowers have an almost otherworldly appearance, and the blossoms often come in shades of green. In these plants, what's typically called a "flower" is really a cluster of colorful, fused bracts; these surround the true flowers, which are tiny and usually insignificant in appearance. When the plants' stems are cut, they exude a milky sap that can irritate eyes and skin.

The following spurges fall into two groups. The first type forms bushy mounds and bears flattened flower heads in late spring and summer; the second, blooming in late winter and spring, sends up numerous leafy, upright stems topped by rounded to dome-shaped blossoms.

Among mounding types is appropriately named cushion spurge, *E. polychroma (E. epithymoides).* Successful in Zones A2, A3, 1–24, 26, 28–45, it forms a dense hemisphere to 1½ feet high, covered with flattened clusters of yellow-and-green flowers. Leaves turn red in fall. Reaching 2 feet tall and wide, *E. dulcis* 'Chameleon' (Zones 2b–24, 31–34) has foliage that emerges purple, matures to bronzy green, then turns purple again in fall; its yellowish green blossoms are tinged with purple.

Of the upright types, *E. × martinii* (Zones 3–24, 31, 32) is

Echinacea purpurea

Euphorbia characias

Geranium × *cantabrigiense* 'Biokovo'

Gypsophila paniculata 'Bristol Fairy'

the shortest at 2½ feet high and wide. Its leaves are bronze tinted, while the chartreuse flowers have brown centers. *E. amygdaloides* (Zones 2b–24, 31–41) may reach 3 feet tall and 1 foot across; its stems and leaf undersides are infused with red. Its selection 'Purpurea' has decidedly purple foliage. *E. characias* grows in Zones 4–24, 31, and warmer parts of 32; it forms a dome-shaped plant 3 to 4 feet high and wide. Among its selections are some with entirely chartreuse flowers, others with brown-centered ones.

GERANIUM
CRANESBILL, GERANIUM
Zones vary. Full sun or light shade; regular water.

Not to be confused with common or garden geranium (*Pelargonium*), these true ("hardy") geraniums all have long-stalked, lobed (maplelike to finely cut) leaves and circular flowers with five petals (more in double-flowered individuals). Sizes vary greatly, but most are spreading to mounding in form, ideal for providing contrast among more rigid-looking individuals and for softening the edges of pathways. Flower colors include white, pink shades, maroon, purple, lavender, and blue. Nurseries offer a great many species and named selections; those presented here are just a sampler.

Among spreading kinds successful in Zones 1–24, 31–43, summer-blooming *G.* × *cantabrigiense* is the lowest, reaching just 6 inches high (but spreading widely). Selections offer ³/₄- to 1-inch blossoms in pink-tinted white and in bright pink. *G. cinereum,* with gray-green foliage, reaches 1 foot high and bears pale pink, 1- to 1½-inch summer flowers. Another 1-footer is *G. himalayense (G. grandiflorum),* with 1½- to 2-inch blue flowers from late spring into summer; its leaves turn red in fall.

Taller, bushier geraniums include the popular *G.* 'Johnson's Blue' (Zones 2–9, 14–24, 30–41), a 1½-foot, mounding plant with intense violet-blue, 2-inch flowers from spring into fall; leaves turn red in autumn. Popular *G. endressii* 'Wargrave Pink' (Zones 1–9, 14–24, 31–43) also reaches 1½ feet and a bit wider, displaying vivid pink, inch-wide blossoms all summer. Variable *G. sanguineum,* to 2½ feet high and somewhat wider, grows in Zones A2, A3, 1–9, 14–24, 30–45; it blooms in spring and summer. Named selections offer 1½-inch flowers in white, pink, and purple.

Most hardy geraniums can remain in place for many years before they begin to decline. When this happens, divide the clumps in early spring.

GYPSOPHILA paniculata
BABY'S BREATH
Zones A2, A3, 1–10, 14–16, 18–21, 31–45, H1. Full sun; moderate water. Self-sower.

Resembling a tumbleweed covered in tiny white blossoms,

frothy baby's breath is the perfect airy, see-through foil to heavier-looking plants with larger leaves and flowers. The basic species makes a mound about 3 feet high and wide—a mass of threadlike, branching stems and $\frac{1}{8}$-inch flowers. More widely grown, though, are various selections with flowers two to three times that size. Double-flowered selections are also popular, as are several compact forms (with single or double flowers in both white and pink) that grow to about half the normal size. Once established, baby's breath is a permanent plant that never needs division.

HEMEROCALLIS

DAYLILY

Zones 1–45, H1, H2. Full sun, except as noted; regular water.

Throughout the growing season, the fountainlike clumps of narrow, arching leaves are good-looking accents in the cottage garden. But from late spring into summer (and, in some selections, again in fall), daylilies come alive with color, bearing showy blossoms mostly in warm colors—yellow, orange, red, cream, pink—as well as in maroon, purple, lavender, and bicolor combinations. Borne on slender, tip-branching stems that rise well above the leaves, the lily-shaped flowers last just one day, but plants produce so many buds that the show goes on for weeks.

Most modern hybrids bear 3- to 8-inch-wide blooms on stems that reach $2\frac{1}{2}$ to 4 feet tall.

Small-growing and "miniature" types may reach no higher than 2 feet when in bloom, bearing correspondingly small blossoms; a few of these, notably yellow-flowered 'Stella de Oro', bloom throughout the growing season. Countless named selections are available, particularly from daylily specialists.

Where summers are hot and dry, plants appreciate a bit of afternoon shade (when you plant, remember that flowers always face the source of light). Divide clumps when they become crowded— in fall or early spring where summers are hot, in summer in cooler regions.

HEUCHERA

CORAL BELLS

Zones vary. Full sun, except as noted; moderate to regular water.

Showy coral bells have long been favorites for the front of the border, where their good-looking foliage and tiny (just $\frac{1}{8}$- to $\frac{1}{4}$-inch), delicate but flashy flowers can be readily appreciated.

H. sanguinea, an old-fashioned cottage garden staple, grows in Zones A1–A3, 1–11, 14–24, 31–45. Its long-stalked, rounded, scallop-edged, 1- to 2-inch leaves form mounded clumps 8 to 12 inches high; starting in spring and extending into summer, thread-thin stems rise to 2 feet, bearing open spikes of nodding bells in bright red to coral pink. The hybrid *H. × brizoides* (Zones 1–10, 14–24, 31–45) is similar in appearance but potentially a

Hemerocallis

Heuchera sanguinea

Iberis sempervirens

Iris, tall bearded, 'Orange Harvest'

Iris, Siberian, 'Silver Edge'

little taller, with stems to 2½ feet high. Named selections of both *H. sanguinea* and *H. × brizoides* offer flowers in white and shades of pink and red.

A separate group of coral bells is grown strictly for foliage beauty (they do produce tall flowering stems in early summer, but the tiny blossoms are drab). Selections of *H. americana* grow 1 to 2 feet high and wide, with large leaves (to 4 inches across) variously marbled and patterned in silver, chocolate, maroon, and green. They grow in Zones 1–9, 14–24, 32–43. The *H. micrantha* selection 'Palace Purple' (Zones 1–10, 14–24, 31–43) grows to 1 by 1½ feet, has 3-inch, maplelike leaves in brownish purple.

Give all kinds of coral bells full sun except where summers are hot and dry; in those areas, they need light or partial shade. Divide crowded clumps in early spring (or in fall, where winters are mild).

IBERIS sempervirens
EVERGREEN CANDYTUFT
Zones 1–24, 31–45. Full sun, except as noted; regular water. Fragrant.

All through spring, evergreen candytuft glistens with a blanket of snowy white blossoms—and the glossy dark green, narrow leaves keep the plant attractive even when it's out of bloom. It's low and broad, reaching 1 foot high and spreading to about twice that wide; the small blossoms are tightly packed into 2-inch-wide,

nearly flat-topped clusters at stem ends. A number of named selections are sold, including smaller-growing plants as well as two varieties ('Autumnale' and 'Autumn Snow') that flower again in fall.

Plant evergreen candytuft in full sun except in hot-summer regions, where it prefers some afternoon shade. When plants decline after several years, replace them with new ones.

IRIS
Zones vary. Full sun, except as noted; water needs vary.

Irises' flat fans of leaves grow in clumps that provide a nice contrast among bushy or mounding plants. Each flower consists of six parts: three upright segments, called standards, and three flaring to drooping ones, called falls. In *bearded* irises, the falls are adorned by a fuzzy-looking, caterpillarlike "beard"; in the *beardless* sort, the beard is lacking. Two types of irises—one from each category—are first-rate choices for the cottage garden.

The irises you'll see most often are the tall bearded kind, successful in Zones 1–24, 30–45. Clumps of swordlike leaves grow up to 2 feet high; branched flower stems rise above them, reaching 2½ to 4 feet. The bloom season extends over 3 to 4 weeks in midspring, and you can choose from varieties that flower early, midseason, and late. Colors include all but true red and spectrum blue, and the available patterns and combinations are nearly infinite. Specialty growers offer a bewildering array of choices; some sell "antique" varieties that are especially appropriate for period gardens.

Among beardless irises, Siberian irises (Zones 1–10, 14–23, 32–45) are the most widely grown. The plants form grassy-looking clumps of very narrow, upright leaves; from these, slim (often unbranched) stems rise 2 to 4 feet high, each bearing several flowers at the top. Colors include violet, wine red, lavender, blue, pink, white, cream, and yellow; bloom time coincides with that of the mid-season tall beardeds.

Irises are happy in full sun except where summers are very hot; there, they appreciate some light shade. Tall bearded irises need regular water from the start of the growing season until 6 weeks after bloom; thereafter, moderate water is sufficient. Give Siberian irises regular water throughout the growing season. When clumps become crowded, divide them: in summer or early fall for bearded irises, in spring or fall for Siberian irises.

LIATRIS spicata

GAYFEATHER

Zones A2, A3, 1–10, 14–24, 26, 28–45. Full sun; moderate to regular water.

On close inspection, you can see that the individual blossoms are small daisies—but in other respects, gayfeather doesn't look much like a daisy relative at all. Its leaves are long and narrow, forming grasslike clumps; from these, flower stems rise to 4 feet high in summer, each ending in a narrow, bottlebrushlike spike of tiny light purple blossoms with prominent stamens. Named selections include shorter individuals and those with flowers in white, lilac, and rose pink. When clumps become crowded after a number of years, divide them in early spring.

LUPINUS

LUPINE

Zones A1–A3, 1–7, 14–17, 34, 36–45. Full sun, except as noted; regular water.

Though they're relatively late arrivals on the scene (the original "classic" hybrids weren't developed until the early 1900s) lupines have become essential components of the English-style cottage garden. Like delphiniums, they're at their magnificent best only in English-type climates featuring cool to mild summers with some cool humidity. In those favored regions, the plants form vigorous, bushy clumps of large, distinctive leaves that resemble a hand with fingers outstretched. From mid- or late spring into summer, foxtail-like spikes tightly packed with sweet pea–shaped flowers rise to 4 to 5 feet; colors include violet, blue, white, pink, red, and yellow, and there are bicolors as well. The Russell Hybrids were the original garden strain,

Liatris spicata

Lupinus, Russell Hybrids

Lychnis coronaria

Paeonia 'Chief Justice'

but newer types (such as the New Generation Hybrids) are more reliable performers. Where summers are warm and dry, give the plants light shade.

Lupines are not long lived. When they decline, replace them with new plants.

LYCHNIS

Zones vary. Full sun or light shade; water needs vary. L. coronaria is a self-sower.

For ease of culture, eye-catching color, and wildflower charm, these plants are "it." They make the greatest impact when planted en masse, but individual plants scattered among other annuals and perennials look just right in a cottage garden.

Summer-blooming Maltese cross, *L. chalcedonica* (Zones A1–A3, 1–10, 14–24, 31–45), has stiffly upright stems clothed in lance-shaped leaves for most of their 2- to 3-foot height. Each stem is topped by a mushroom-shaped cluster of $1/2$-inch, blazing scarlet flowers with fringed petals (for the faint of heart, there's also a white-flowered form). Give this species regular water; when clumps become crowded, divide and replant them in early spring.

The many common names of *L. coronaria*—crown pink, mullein pink, rose campion—testify to its widespread popularity. White stems to $2\frac{1}{2}$ feet high rise from a clump of silvery white, woolly, oval leaves; from late spring into summer, each

stem bears at its tip clusters of circular, 1-inch blossoms in an assertive magenta. Available selections offer other flower colors, among them pure white and pinkish white with a red central eye. Successful in Zones 1–9, 14–24, 30, 32, 34–43, crown pink is quite short lived as a perennial—but it self-seeds freely, ensuring you a steady supply of replacement plants. It does best with moderate water.

PAEONIA

PEONY

Zones A1–A3, 1–11, 14–20, 30–45. Full sun; regular water. Fragrant.

Magnificent peonies offer sumptuous, fragrant blossoms on handsome plants with the bulk of shrubs. Each year, new shoots rise from bare earth in early spring, then develop into bushy plants (to 2 to 4 feet high and wide) clothed in large, many-segmented leaves. In mid- to late spring, round buds appear at the stem ends and open into satiny blossoms up to 10 inches across. Flowers may be single, semidouble, or double; colors include red, pink shades, white, cream, and yellow. Specialists offer a wide array of named selections.

These perennials need winter chill to perform well. In the warmer zones listed above, consult a specialty catalog and select those varieties that need the least amount of chilling for successful bloom. Peonies are long-lived plants that never need division.

PENSTEMON

Zones vary. Full sun; regular water.

These showy perennials typically make clumps of upright, leafy stems topped with spikes of tubular to bell-shaped blossoms in spring and summer. The many penstemons native to arid and semiarid parts of the U. S. are first-rate choices for long-term color in their preferred climes, but they do poorly in hot, humid regions and with regular watering. The following three penstemons, however, tolerate a range of climates and flourish in normal garden conditions.

P. × gloxinioides is perennial only in Zones 6–9, 12–24. It's a compact, bushy 2- to 4-footer with bell-shaped, 2-inch-long flowers. Named selections come in lavender, purple, violet, red, pink, and white; the colored flowers often have white throats. *P. barbatus* (Zones 1–20, 31–43) is an upright, open-structured plant to 3 feet high and about half that wide, with narrow, bell-like pink to red flowers to 1 1/2 inches long. Named selections and strains offer a greater color range, including lavender, purple, and yellow. Robust *P. digitalis,* successful in Zones 1–9, 14–24, 29–43, reaches 3 to 5 feet tall and 2 to 3 feet wide, bearing clusters of white or pale pink, 1-inch bells. Its selection 'Husker Red' has maroon foliage.

Penstemons tend to decline after a few years; at that point, remove them and start over with new plants.

PRIMULA
PRIMROSE

Zones vary. Full sun to partial shade; regular water. P. vulgaris *is fragrant.*

Among the multitudes of lovely primroses, two similar types are special favorites for cottage gardens. Both make low clumps of tongue- to paddle-shaped, wrinkled leaves.

The classic English primrose (the cowslip of homemade cowslip wine) is *P. vulgaris (P. acaulis),* successful in Zones A3, 2–6, 14–17, 21–24, 32–41. Its leaves reach 10 inches long; in early spring, stems rise just high enough to raise the 1 1/4-inch, fragrant yellow flowers above the foliage. The species bears one flower per stem, but garden strains may carry several blossoms on each stem—and in addition to yellow, they offer blossoms in white, red, bronze tones, and blue, all with a yellow central eye.

More widely grown is *P. × polyantha,* polyanthus primrose (sometimes also called English primrose), a hybrid group successful in Zones 1–24, 32–41. Leaves grow to 8 inches long; in midwinter to early or midspring, 8 to 12-inch flower stems rise above the foliage clumps, bearing many-flowered clusters of 1- to 2-inch, yellow-centered blossoms in an amazing color range that includes everything but true green and black.

When clumps eventually decline and begin to bloom less profusely, divide them as soon as flowering finishes.

Penstemon barbatus 'Elfin Pink'

Primula vulgaris

Salvia nemorosa 'Ostfriesland'

Scabiosa columbaria 'Butterfly Blue'

SALVIA

SAGE

Zones 2–10, 14–24, 30–41. Full sun; regular water.

These easy-to-grow plants are a natural fit for cottage gardens. Dozens of species and hybrids are available—especially to gardeners in the Southwest and West, where native sages and those from Mexico thrive. Among the many choices are three old favorites that succeed in a broad range of climates: *S. nemorosa, S. × superba,* and *S. × sylvestris.* They're so similar that there's some name confusion in the nursery trade. All form low, spreading foliage rosettes that send up branched, somewhat leafy, 2- to 3-foot flower stems bearing narrow spires of ½-inch flowers over a long summer-into-fall period. Purple, blue violet, pink, and white are the typical colors. Divide crowded clumps in spring.

SCABIOSA

PINCUSHION FLOWER

Zones vary. Full sun, except as noted; moderate to regular water.

The perennial pincushion flowers have the same slightly domed flower heads as their annual kin (see page 48), but their color range is more limited and the plants are shorter. The two commonly available species both bloom in spring and summer, sending up flowering stems to about 2 feet high that bear 3-inch-wide clusters of blossoms in blue shades, pink, or white. Both

form clumps of narrow leaves, but foliage of *S. caucasica* (Zones 1–10, 14–24, 32–43) may be smooth edged or finely cut, while that of *S. columbaria* (Zones 2–11, 14–24, 32–35) is gray green and finely cut. *S. caucasica* is best suited to regions with cool to mild summers, where it can grow in full sun; elsewhere, it performs better with light shade. *S. columbaria* is the better choice for hot-summer regions—and where winters are mild, its bloom can extend into fall.

Divide crowded clumps of either species in spring.

SEDUM

STONECROP

Zones vary. Full sun; regular water.

These succulents are a varied bunch, including favorite rock garden and container plants. The following three trouble-free, vigorous sorts are especially good choices for the cottage garden, offering interest throughout the growing season. In spring, clumps of ground-level buds give rise to fleshy, upright stems set with rubbery, oval leaves. Bloom begins in mid- to late summer, when large, domed to flat-topped clusters of tiny star-shaped blossoms appear at the stem ends. When flowering is over, the stems die but remain upright; the blossoms, too, hang on, drying to bronze or maroon and providing attractive material for dried floral arrangements.

S. spectabile (Hylotelephium spectabile) succeeds in Zones

1–24, 28–43; it grows about 1½ feet high and has blue-green leaves and 6-inch clusters of pink flowers. Named selections come in white, deep rose, and muted red shades. The very similar *S. telephium (Hylotelephium telephium),* suited to Zones 1–24, 29–43, differs largely in its narrower, gray-green leaves and purplish pink blossoms; it's also a bit taller, reaching as high as 2 feet. It has a number of named selections with foliage tinged or variegated in red, burgundy, or pink. A hybrid of the preceding two species is the widely sold *S.* 'Autumn Joy' (*Hylotelephium* 'Autumn Joy', *H.* 'Herbstfreude'), successful in Zones 1–10, 14–24, 29–43. It's a 1½- to 2-foot-tall plant with blue-green leaves and 4- to 5-inch-wide clusters of pink flowers.

The stonecrops can remain in place for a number of years, until floppy stems and a decrease in bloom indicate overcrowding. When this occurs, dig and divide the clumps in early spring.

STACHYS
Zones 1–24, 29–43. Full sun or light shade, except as noted; moderate water.

The following two species don't look much alike, but they do share one key trait: ease of growth. Lamb's ears, *S. byzantina (S. lanata, S. olympica),* gets its common name from its elongated, furry white leaves. A single plant soon spreads into a foliage patch about 6 inches high. In late spring to early summer, flower

stems clothed in small leaves rise to 1½ feet, bearing tiers of small lavender blossoms. Named selections include a larger-leafed type, a nonblooming variety ('Silver Carpet'), and 'Primrose Heron', with chartreuse leaves coated in the typical white "fur."

Though strictly decorative today, wood betony, *S. officinalis,* had a medieval career as a medicinal herb. It forms a tight clump of long-stalked, oblong, heavily veined green leaves; midsummer flower stems, each bearing several pairs of smaller leaves, reach 2 to 3 feet and terminate in narrow spikes of small reddish purple blossoms.

Both species take full sun or light shade except in hot-summer regions, where they need afternoon shade to do well. When performance declines, divide clumps in spring (*S. byzantina* will need division more often than *S. officinalis*).

VIOLA odorata
SWEET VIOLET
Zones 1–24, 29–43. Partial to full shade, except as noted; regular water. Fragrant.

Ideal for softening pathway edges, sweet violet produces 4- to 8-inch-high foliage clumps that spread by strawberrylike runners. In late winter or early spring, scented inch-wide flowers in purple, blue shades, pink, or white peek from amid the long-stalked, nearly circular leaves. The plant will take full sun in cool-summer regions.

Sedum 'Autumn Joy'

Stachys byzantina

Viola odorata 'White Czar'

S H R U B S

Here are the familiar woody, bushy plants that retain their branch structure throughout the year. Plant them once and they're yours for life! In these pages, we focus on deciduous and evergreen shrubs treasured for their seasonal display of blossoms and, often, for their fragrance as well. (For information on that most popular of flowering shrubs, the rose, turn to page 94.)

Buddleja davidii

Caryopteris × clandonensis 'Dark Knight'

Deutzia gracilis

BUDDLEJA
BUTTERFLY BUSH
Zones vary. Full sun or light shade; moderate to regular water. Deciduous. Fragrant.

Large, open, arching shrubs with narrow leaves, buddlejas flower profusely in spring or summer, depending on the type. For spring bloom, *B. alternifolia* puts on a real show in Zones 2b–24, 28–39. Small clusters of lavender flowers cover the stems after leaves have formed; plants reach 12 feet high and wide and can be trained into small trees. Summer-flowering *B. davidii* (Zones 2–24, 28–41, H1) can grow 10 feet tall and wide. Small blossoms are packed into foxtail-like clusters at stem ends; the flowers are typically lilac with an orange eye, but named selections come in white, lavender to purple, pink, and wine red. Available varieties include 'Harlequin', with variegated foliage and deep violet blooms, and a number of smaller (3- to 6-foot) choices.

CARYOPTERIS × clandonensis
BLUE MIST
Zones 2b–9, 14–24, 29–41. Full sun; moderate water. Deciduous.

Here's a narrow-leafed, small shrub—just 2 feet high and wide—for planting among fore-ground perennials and annuals, where it contributes a cooling blue haze to the midsummer garden. At bloom time, clusters of small blossoms with prominent stamens appear near the stem tips. Named selections offer specific blue shades; 'Worcester Gold' features pale blue blossoms arrayed against chartreuse foliage.

DEUTZIA
Zones 2–11, 14–17, 29–41. Full sun or light shade; regular water. Deciduous.

Deutzias come into bloom at tulip time in late spring, covering themselves in clouds of clustered, starlike white or pink flowers just $1/2$ to $3/4$ inch wide. All have lance-shaped to oval leaves.

Slender deutzia, *D. gracilis*, with pure white blooms, is an arching shrub that may attain 6 feet but typically grows no larger than 4 feet high and wide. Its selection 'Nikko' reaches just 2 feet tall but spreads to 5 feet across. The *D. × elegantissima* selections vary in habit from upright to arching, in height from 4 to 6 feet; they bear flowers in white and shades of pink. Upright *D. scabra* is the tallest deutzia, reaching 7 to 10 feet high and up to 6 feet wide; its selections offer double blossoms (in both white and pink) and variegated foliage.

HIBISCUS syriacus
ROSE OF SHARON, SHRUB ALTHAEA
Zones 2–24, northern 26, 28–41, H1.
Full sun; regular water. Deciduous.

Resembling a bush adorned with hollyhocks *(Alcea),* rose of Sharon enlivens the garden from mid- or late summer until frost. Its 2$\frac{1}{2}$- to 4-inch blossoms may be single, semidouble, or double; colors are white, lavender, purple, red, and pink, often with a contrasting red or purple throat. Thickly clothed in oval or lobed leaves with coarsely toothed edges, the plants typically reach about 12 feet tall; they're narrowly upright when young, wider and more spreading with age. Older named selections form seed capsules that lead to crops of volunteer seedlings; to avoid this, choose the newer seedless triploid hybrids, such as pure white 'Diana'.

KOLKWITZIA amabilis
BEAUTY BUSH
Zones 2–11, 14–20, 31–41. Full
sun or partial shade; regular water.
Deciduous.

For a striking fountain of pink bloom, beauty bush can't be beat. In mid- to late spring, the 10- to 12-foot tall, vase-shaped plant smothers itself in clusters of inch-long, bell-shaped blossoms in light pink with yellow throats. Pinkish brown, bristly fruits appear after the flowers fade, prolonging the color display (but in a more subtle fashion). The oval gray-green leaves turn yellow or red in fall.

PHILADELPHUS
MOCK ORANGE
Zones vary. Full sun, except as noted;
moderate to regular water.
Deciduous. Fragrant (some).

The scent of orange blossom does, indeed, waft from some of these old-fashioned favorites. But scented or no, all put on a lavish late spring or early summer show of lovely white blossoms that almost obscure the foliage.

The *P.* × *lemoinei* hybrids (Zones 2b–17, 30–34, 39) include both single- and double-blossomed selections, most bearing 1-inch flowers on mounding plants to 6 feet high and wide. Among the selections of *P.* × *virginalis* (Zones A3, 1a, 2–17, 30–41) are choices offering single or double flowers to 2 inches across. Plant size varies; some attain 8 feet tall and broad, while others reach just 3 to 4 feet in both directions.

Sweet mock orange, *P. coronarius* (Zones A1–A3, 1a, 2–24, 30–41), offers guaranteed fragrance from 1$\frac{1}{2}$-inch flowers on an upright, arching bush to 12 feet high and wide.

Mock oranges prefer full sun except in the hottest climates, where partial shade is better.

PHLOMIS fruticosa
JERUSALEM SAGE
Zones 3b–24, 31, warmer 32. Full
sun; little to moderate water.
Evergreen.

Bold foliage and bright flowers make Jerusalem sage a garden

Hibiscus syriacus

Kolkwitzia amabilis

Philadelphus coronarius

Phlomis fruticosa

Spiraea prunifolia 'Plena'

Spiraea japonica 'Alpina'

standout. Plants reach about 4 feet high and wide, the stems bearing woolly-textured gray-green, arrowhead-shaped leaves to 4 inches long and just over an inch wide. Ball-shaped whorls of bright yellow, 1-inch flowers appear in tiers along the upper half of the stems. The hybrid *P.* 'Edward Bowles' has bolder leaves—to 6 inches long and 3 inches wide—and larger flower clusters; it's often sold simply as *P. fruticosa*. Both flower in mid- to late spring and will bloom again one or more times during summer if plants are cut back lightly after each round of blossoms.

SPIRAEA

Zones vary. Full sun or light shade; moderate to regular water. Deciduous.

The popular "bridal wreath" spiraeas are small-leafed plants with arching stems that are covered at bloom time in clusters of small (less than $^1/_2$-inch) white blossoms. The group includes several species and named selections. Earliest to bloom is *S. prunifolia* 'Plena', shoe button or bridal wreath spiraea (Zones A2, A3, 2–11, 14–21, 31–41), bearing double flowers in late winter to midspring (depending on climate), before the leaves emerge. Reaching 6 to 8 feet tall and almost as wide, the plant is a broad-based clump of slender, upright-arching stems; the foliage turns red in fall.

Other bridal wreath spiraeas flower in late spring and even

into summer. *S.* × *vanhouttei* (Zones A1–A3, 1–11, 14–21, 29–45) is an arching, fountainlike shrub to 6 feet high and 8 feet across, with leaves that may turn purplish in fall. *S. nipponica* 'Snowmound' (Zones 1–11, 14–21, 32–43) is similar but smaller, to just 3 feet tall by 5 feet wide, and its leaves offer little or no fall color.

Shrubbier than the bridal wreath types are several pink-flowered spiraeas. These are upright to mounding plants that succeed in Zones A2, A3, 2–10, 14–21, 31–43. All are selections of *S. japonica,* though many may still be sold under a former name, *S.* × *bumalda.* Blossoms in various pink shades come in broad, flattened clusters from summer into fall; the leaves turn bronzy red to purplish before dropping. Among named selections, the smallest are $1^1/_2$ to 2 feet high and wide, the tallest about 5 feet. Several have chartreuse leaves that hold their color until fall; others have maroon-tinted foliage for part or all of the growing season.

SYRINGA vulgaris

COMMON LILAC

Zones A1–A3, 1–22, 32–45. Full sun, except as noted; regular water. Deciduous. Fragrant.

Once experienced, the heady fragrance of lilacs is never forgotten. That perfume—and the loveliness of the brief spring bloom—have endeared these shrubs to generations of gardeners. Left unpruned, the plants form bulky clumps of stems that build to a height of 10 or even 20 feet and spread to at least half that wide. In midspring, small blossoms packed into cone-shaped spikes appear at branch ends; colors include white, many purple shades (from pale lavender to deepest violet), pink, cream, and even bicolors.

Give lilacs a lightly shaded location in hot-summer climates. Out of bloom, they're undistinguished plants with ordinary broad, oval leaves, so place them where their springtime scent can be enjoyed but where they won't dominate the scene all season. They definitely need at least some winter chill to flower well. In the warmer parts of their range (Zones 12–16, 18–22), you'll have the best success with the various Descanso Hybrids; 'Lavender Lady' is the most widely sold choice.

VIBURNUM

Zones vary. Full sun or partial shade; regular water. Deciduous. V. × carlcephalum is fragrant.

Of the many viburnums, the old-fashioned spring-blooming "snowball" types are cottage garden favorites. Several species bear the classic ball-shaped clusters of flat single blossoms; all bloom after coming into leaf.

Fragrant snowball, *V. × carlcephalum* (Zones 3–11, 14–24, 31–34, 39), grows 6 to 10 feet high and wide. Its sweetly scented blossoms come in larger clusters (4 to 5 inches across) than

those of other snowball types. Leaves are dull gray green, turning reddish purple in fall.

Common snowball, *V. opulus* 'Roseum' ('Sterile'), succeeds in Zones A2, A3, 1–9, 14–24, 29–43; it reaches 8 to 15 feet high and wide, with arching branches bearing 2½-inch blossom clusters. The maplelike leaves turn yellow, red, or reddish purple in fall.

Japanese snowball, *V. plicatum* (Zones 3–9, 14–24, 31–35, 37, 39), also grows 8 to 15 feet high and wide, but its branches are carried in nearly horizontal tiers, giving the plant a layered look. The 3-inch flower clusters look like those of *V. opulus* 'Roseum'; leaves turn purplish red in fall.

WEIGELA

Zones 1–11, 14–21, 32–41. Full sun or light shade; regular water. Deciduous.

In spring, these easy-to-grow shrubs transform themselves into lush mounds of color. Resembling inch-long foxgloves (*Digitalis*), the funnel-shaped flowers appear singly and in clusters all along the leafed-out stems.

W. florida is an arching plant to 10 feet high and a bit wider. The species bears pink to rosy red flowers; named selections come in white and pink shades. The various hybrid weigelas are generally shorter plants, reaching just 5 to 7 feet. They offer blossoms in white, pink, and red, and you'll also find forms with purple, yellow, or variegated leaves.

Syringa vulgaris 'Paul Thirion'

Viburnum opulus 'Roseum'

Weigela florida 'Minuet'

V I N E S

Vines are those plants that don't seem to know when to stop growing: their stems continue to elongate for much of the growing season, yet they don't have enough "starch" to hold themselves upright. Instead, they rely on the support of a fence, trellis, or even a nearby shrub or tree, climbing by any of several means—twining stems, holdfast disks, coiling leafstalks or tendrils, or simple scrambling. (For more on the best-known scramblers—climbing roses—turn to page 94.) On these pages, we describe both annual vines and longer-lived woody ones.

Ipomoea nil, Early Call strain

Lathyrus odoratus

ANNUAL VINES

Like their nonvining kin (see pages 42–49), annual vines are fast growers that complete their life cycle within a single growing season.

IPOMOEA
MORNING GLORY
All zones. Full sun; moderate to regular water. Warm season.

Country gardens and morning glories go hand in hand. Given strings or wire to climb, the twining vines ascend vigorously to a height of 10 to 15 feet, covering their support with heart-shaped leaves. The 3- to 4-inch, broadly funnel-shaped flowers look like old-time gramophone speakers; blue is the most familiar color, but several other hues are available. As the common name suggests, the blossoms open in the morning but close by the afternoon.

The old-fashioned favorite is *I. tricolor,* blooming from summer until frost. Sky blue 'Heavenly Blue' is the traditional variety, but you'll also find choices in white or magenta; all typically have a white or yellow throat. Summer-blooming *I. nil* is similar, featuring selections in red ('Scarlett O'Hara') and rosy tan ('Chocolate') as well as a mixed-color strain in blue, white, lavender, pink, and magenta. Plant seeds outdoors after the last-frost date; or, where the growing season is short, start seeds indoors for planting out as soon as the danger of frost is past.

LATHYRUS odoratus
SWEET PEA
All zones. Full sun; regular water. Cool season. Fragrant.

The fresh, sweet fragrance alone would assure sweet peas' place in the hearts of gardeners—but as a bonus, that delightful perfume is carried by lovely, showy blossoms in cream, white, blue, purple, violet, red, pink, and various bicolor combinations. Borne in long-stemmed clusters, the flowers come on tendril-climbing vines that need the support of strings or wire mesh to achieve their mature height of 5 feet or more. Many strains of these cool-season annuals are sold; choose those which best suit your climate.

In mild-winter regions with warm to hot summers, early-flowering strains are best. Spring-flowering strains succeed where spring is cool to moderately warm, as well as in short-season, cool- to moderate-summer regions (in short-season areas, they'll bloom primarily in summer). Summer-flowering strains are somewhat heat resistant, but they perform best where summers are cool to fairly warm (not hot). For all types, sow seeds directly in the garden, following the instructions on the seed packet for timing.

TROPAEOLUM majus

NASTURTIUM

All zones. Full sun or light shade; regular water. Cool season. Self-sower.

Traditional vining nasturtiums (for bush types, see page 48) ascend to about 6 feet, climbing by coiling their leafstalks around strings or wire. If you don't give them a support, they're quite happy to thread their way through neighboring plants or spread to form an impromptu flowering ground cover. However you choose to use them, they offer bright colors and distinctive form.

Set off against a backdrop of long-stalked, nearly circular leaves are five-lobed, trumpetlike flowers to about 2½ inches across, in orange, yellow, red, creamy white, maroon, and mahogany. And in true cottage garden tradition, nasturtiums grace the table with more than bouquets: the young leaves, flowers, and unripe seeds are all edible, adding a peppery tang to salads.

Where winters are cold, plant seeds directly in the garden early in spring, as soon as the danger of frost is past. In mild-winter, hot-summer regions, sow in fall for winter and spring bloom.

WOODY VINES

Compared to annual vines, woody kinds are more like runaway shrubs—once you plant them, they'll live for years.

CLEMATIS

Zones 1–9, 14–17, 19–23, 31–41, except as noted. Full sun or partial shade; regular water. Deciduous.

The wide world of clematis includes numerous species and named selections, but the large-flowered hybrids dominate the nursery and garden scene. Their 5- to 10-inch blossoms are truly magnificent, guaranteed to elicit gasps of admiration. Petal-like structures called tepals stand in for actual petals; elongated and pointed, they form flat, circular blossoms in a wide assortment of cool colors—blue, lavender, purple, maroon, crimson, and pink—as well as pure white and some bicolors. Double-flowered kinds exist, bearing blossoms so full of pointed "petals" that they resemble small dahlias. Most are sold simply by cultivar name— 'Ramona', for example. The *C. × jackmanii* hybrids, which often bear names that make note of the parent species (e.g. 'Jackmanii Rubra', 'Jackmanii Alba'), take a bit more cold than most other large-flowered types, growing in Zones A2, A3, 42, and 43 in addition to those listed above.

Clematis vines are slender stemmed, climbing by twining leafstalks; the leaves have three elongated oval to heart-shaped

Tropaeolum majus

Clematis 'Comtesse de Bouchard'

Lonicera sempervirens

Lonicera × heckrottii

Vitis

leaflets, each on a long stalk. Expect the plants to reach a height of 8 to 15 feet with the support of wire or strings; if shrubs or small trees are within reach, the growing clematis stems are likely to attach to their branches as well.

LONICERA
HONEYSUCKLE
Zones vary. Full sun or partial shade; moderate water. Deciduous and evergreen. Fragrant (some).

Honeysuckles and fragrance seem almost synonymous—so it comes as a surprise to find that some kinds have no scent at all. Even so, all of these twining vines provide colorful, easy-to-grow garden decoration. There are two flower types: one sort is a slender tube that resembles a firecracker, while the other is a trumpet that flares into upper and lower lips.

Among the types with two-lipped blossoms is rampant *L. japonica*—intensely fragrant, but so invasive that it's best avoided. A good substitute for it is woodbine, *L. periclymenum* (Zones 1–24, 30–41), which twines to 10 to 20 feet and is evergreen where winters are very mild. In summer and fall, 2-inch blossoms—purple on the outside, creamy white within—perfume the air. These are followed by a crop of showy red berries. Named selections offer purple-and-yellow, red-and-cream, and solid yellow blooms.

Gold flame honeysuckle, *L. × heckrottii* (Zones 2–24, 30–39, H1, H2), grows at a moderate pace to 10 to 15 feet. Lightly scented, 2-inch flowers in yellow and coral pink bloom from midspring until frost. The plant is evergreen in warm-winter regions, deciduous elsewhere.

Honeysuckles with tubular, firecrackerlike flowers include trumpet honeysuckle, *L. sempervirens* (Zones 2–41); despite its botanical name, it's evergreen only in the mildest-winter areas. The 10- to 20-foot plant is decked out in 2-inch, scentless orange-red flowers from late spring into summer; red berries follow in fall. Yellow- and red-flowered selections are sold. For a similar but hardier vine, look for deciduous *L. × brownii* (Zones A3, 1–7, 31–45). Unscented bright red flowers come over a longer season—late spring to frost—on a smaller (9- to 10-foot) plant.

VITIS
GRAPE
Zones vary. Full sun or partial shade; moderate to regular water. Deciduous.

Since ancient times, grapevines have provided not only crops of delicious fruit, but also handsome foliage and—when grown on an arbor—cooling summer shade. The large, lobed leaves are roughly triangular in outline, with coarsely toothed edges; they often take on brilliant colors in fall. These vigorous vines climb by means of tendrils that wrap securely around supports (including the branches of shrubs and trees). It's best to plant them against a sturdy trellis or arbor, since mature plants become quite heavy, forming a thick trunk with shredding bark.

The many named grape varieties can be loosely divided into two groups: table grapes (larger-fruited types grown for eating fresh) and wine grapes. Consult your local Cooperative Extension Office for advice on the best choices for reliable fruit production in your area.

Among table grapes, the American and American hybrid types include the most cold-hardy varieties; of these, 'Valiant' will even grow in Zones A2 and A3, but the hardiest among the others cannot take regions colder than Zone 2. European varieties are suited only to the West Coast. In the South, muscadine varieties, derived from native species, stand up to the summer heat and humidity.

WISTERIA

Zones vary. Exposure needs vary; little to moderate water. Deciduous. Fragrant.

Wisterias are about equal parts elegance and romance. Whether draping a pergola or framing a window, a vine in full bloom presents a vision of loveliness, a portrait of sensuous floral abundance that's enhanced by the blossoms' sweet, pervasive perfume. And thanks to long leaves composed of numerous narrow leaflets, the graceful look persists for months after the flowers have faded and fallen.

Be aware that wisterias are *big* vines, aggressively twining around anything nearby—including themselves—for support, and that any attempt to keep them heavily restricted will be a full-time job. (Maintaining a plant as a "tree" is about the only worthwhile attempt at major size control.) Plant them only where they have room to develop; as the trunk and limb structure gain size, they too become part of the vine's exceptional beauty.

Two species account for most garden wisterias. Japanese wisteria, *W. floribunda,* grows in Zones 2–24, 26, 28–41. It has the longer flower clusters (to about 1½ feet), with flowers opening progressively from the base (stem end) to the tip. Named selections come in white and many shades of violet, from light to dark; there's also a variety with double lavender flowers. Leaves emerge while the plants are in bloom. Give this species full sun.

Blossom clusters of Chinese wisteria, *W. sinensis* (Zones 3–24, 26, 28–35, 37, 39), are a bit shorter (reaching only 1 foot long), but a vine in bloom still makes quite an impact—all the flowers open at the same time, and they precede the leaves. Light lavender is the standard color. Named selections chosen for beauty and cluster length are your best bet; colors include white, lavender to violet, and pink. Chinese wisteria thrives in both full sun and partial shade.

Wisteria floribunda

Wisteria sinensis

T R E E S

In the original cottage gardens, trees were planted to provide fruits or nuts for the cottager's table. Today, though, the focus has shifted to beauty—and the trees described on these pages deliver an annual floral display well worth a year's wait. Fortunately, some do double duty: apple and crabapple (Malus), plum (Prunus), and pear (Pyrus) all offer tempting fruit as well as flowers.

Cercis canadensis

Cornus florida

CERCIS canadensis
EASTERN REDBUD
Zones 1–24, 26, 28–41. Full sun; moderate to regular water. Deciduous.

A redbud in bloom is a truly gaudy sight. Small, sweet pea–shaped flowers in vivid purplish pink literally cover the tree in early spring, appearing in small clusters on twigs, branches, main limbs, and sometimes even on the trunk. As the blossoms fade, the 3- to 6-inch-long leaves emerge—almost round, with a heart-shaped base and pointed tip. They turn yellow in fall. The round-headed tree reaches 25 to 35 feet tall and wide; in mature specimens, branches are often held in horizontal layers. Named selections offer other flower colors (white, pure pink) and double blossoms; 'Forest Pansy' has wine purple foliage.

CORNUS florida
FLOWERING DOGWOOD
Zones 2b–9, 14–16, northern 26, 28, 29, 31–41. Full sun or light shade; regular water. Deciduous.

Soft and billowy, a blooming dogwood recalls an earthbound cloud. Covering the tree in early to midspring, the showy, 3- to 4-inch blossoms each have four large, petal-like bracts that surround the insignificant true flowers. Named selections are available with bracts in white, pink shades, and rosy red, and you'll also find several choices with variegated foliage. Clusters of berry-like fruits follow the flowers and turn red in fall, as do the oval, 6-inch leaves. Flowering dogwood tends to branch low; its branches are fairly horizontal, with upturned tips. In age, it has a broadly pyramidal but flat-topped silhouette. Mature trees may occasionally reach 40 feet high and wide, but 20 to 30 feet is a more typical size.

CRATAEGUS
HAWTHORN
Zones vary. Full sun; moderate water. Deciduous.

Hawthorns provide striking beauty at two times of year: once as the growing season begins, again as it draws to a close. In midspring, clusters of typically white blossoms less than an inch across burst forth all along the leafed-out branches. After the flowers fade, pendent clusters of small, applelike fruits appear; they ripen in late summer to fall. Many different hawthorns are sold; all are small to medium-size trees, and most have thorny branches. Leaves range from 2 to 4 inches long.

Carriere hawthorn, *C. × lavallei,* grows in Zones 3–12, 14–21, 29–35, 37, 39; it's upright and open, to 25 feet high and no more than 20 feet wide. The tooth-edged leaves turn bronzy red in fall and last into winter, as do the orange-red fruits. English hawthorn, *C. laevigata* (Zones A2, A3, 2–12, 14–17, 28, 30–41), is a fairly twiggy tree to 25 feet high and 20 feet wide, with tiny red fruits and lobed leaves that turn tawny yellow in fall. Named selections include 'Paul's Scarlet', with double blossoms in bright crimson; there are also fruitless forms with white or pink double flowers.

Washington thorn, *C. phaenopyrum* (Zones 2–12, 14–17, 28, 30–41), is about the same size and shape as *C. laevigata,* but it's more open, and its maplelike leaves turn brilliant orange and red in fall. White flowers are followed by showy red fruits that hang on well into winter.

LAGERSTROEMIA indica

CRAPE MYRTLE

Zones 6-10, 12–31, warmer 32, H1, H2. Full sun; moderate water. Deciduous.

Flashy crape myrtle saves its display for summer and early fall, late enough to avoid most of the competition. Trees can reach 25 feet high and nearly as wide, with one or several trunks; the bark is beautifully mottled in light brown and pinkish white. Small oval leaves make a brilliant fall display in yellow, orange, or red. The real show,

though, is in the flowers: small, crepe-papery blooms that appear in large clusters at branch tips from mid- to late summer until frost. Colors run from white through vibrant pink, red, magenta, and purple; many named selections are sold. Also available are a number of *L. indica* hybrids; these have the beauty of *L. indica,* with the bonus of increased hardiness and mildew resistance. Most bear the names of native American tribes ('Chickasaw' and 'Hopi', for example).

MAGNOLIA

Zones vary. Full sun or partial shade; regular water. Deciduous and evergreen.

Elegant, impressive magnolias embrace a wide range of plants, from large shrubs to truly massive trees. Most are deciduous, but there are evergreen sorts as well. Common to all are large, waxy-petaled blossoms and 6- to 8-inch, broadly oval leaves.

Two smaller deciduous magnolias nicely suit a cottage garden scheme. Kobus magnolia, *M. kobus* (Zones 2b–9, 14–24, 32–41), bears lightly fragrant white, 4-inch-wide blossoms on bare branches in early to mid-spring, before leaves emerge. In time, it becomes a fairly upright specimen to 30 feet high and 20 feet wide. Its hybrid *M.* 'Wada's Memory' reaches about the same size, but it grows faster and has slightly larger blooms.

Saucer magnolia, *M. × soulangeana,* succeeds in Zones

Crataegus laevigata 'Paul's Scarlet'

Lagerstroemia indica

Magnolia × soulangeana

Malus (crabapple)

Prunus serrulata (flowering cherry)

2b–10, 12–24, 28–41. Many selections of this popular tree are sold, all with goblet-shaped blossoms to 6 inches or wider, in colors ranging from white through pink to purplish red (and some bicolors). The blossoms appear in early spring, before leaves emerge (look for those that bloom near the end of this period if you live where late frosts are common). Saucer magnolia serves as an ever-enlarging, typically multi-trunked shrub for many years but eventually becomes a large, gray-barked specimen tree to 25 feet high and wide.

MALUS

APPLE and CRABAPPLE

Zones vary. Full sun; moderate to regular water. Deciduous.

Apples and crabapples represent different branches of the same family tree. The ubiquitous eating apples have the sweetest and largest fruits: $2\frac{1}{2}$ to 4 inches in diameter, depending on the variety. Edible crabapples, largely derived from different species than apples, produce applelike but less-sweet fruits in the $1\frac{1}{2}$- to 2-inch range. The various flowering crabapples also bear fruit, but because it is small and typically unpalatable, these trees have a strictly decorative use.

Most crabapples grow in Zones 1–11, 14–21, 29–43, though a few hardier selections are available. Their landscape value is in the masses of 1- to $1\frac{3}{4}$-inch flowers that deck the branches before leaves emerge,

as well as in the fruits that follow. Blossoms come in white, pink shades, and rosy red; they're single in fruiting crabapples, but ornamental types may also have semidouble or double blooms. The fruits are yellow, orange, or red. Most crabapples are small to medium-size trees; the largest may reach 25 feet high and wide. Fall color is rarely notable.

Among apples, adaptability varies considerably. A few varieties will grow in Alaska, a number can thrive in chilly Zone 43, and still others are perfectly suited to virtually frost-free regions of Southern California and Florida. Reaching about 25 feet high and wide, the sturdy-limbed trees are glorious in their mid-spring display of single flowers in delicately pink-tinged white—the well-known "apple blossom pink." In autumn, leaves turn yellow to tawny gold.

When you select apples and crabapples, key your choice to local conditions. For apples, consider both inherent hardiness and how well the tree will bear fruit in your climate; for crabapples, think about resistance to the standard crabapple diseases present in your area. For advice on varieties likely to succeed for you, consult your Cooperative Extension Office.

PRUNUS

FLOWERING CHERRY and FLOWERING PLUM

Zones vary. Full sun; moderate to regular water. Deciduous.

Flowering plums announce spring in lush clouds of white or pink.

Just a bit later in the season, flowering cherries put on a show in the same colors, their dainty blossoms setting the standard for grace and elegance.

Flowering cherries offer quite a wide choice of species, named selections, and named hybrids. Hardiness varies. The most cold-tolerant choices can grow in areas as cold as Zones 2 and 41; at the mild-winter end of the scale, most grow in Zones 3–7, 14–20 in the West, and a few succeed in Zone 31 in the East (though Zones 32–34 are more typical limits). Some are upright, others quite spreading; a few are even arching or weeping. Most have attractive bark and offer some fall foliage color. Flowers, often borne in drooping clusters, may be single, semidouble, or double, from 1 to $2\frac{1}{2}$ inches across.

The flowering plums are a much smaller group. The most widely sold choices are bronze- to purple-leafed selections of myrobalan plum, *P. cerasifera* (Zones 3–22, 28, 31–34, 39). Heights vary from 15 to 40 feet; habits range from upright to rounded and spreading. The inch-wide blossoms are pure white in green-foliaged species, light pink to nearly white in the colored-leaf selections. Most flowering plums produce a crop of edible cherry-size fruits. If you prefer a virtually nonfruiting variety, consider *P. × blireiana* (Zones 3–22, 32–34, 39), a hybrid with double pink blooms and leaves that are reddish purple when new, maturing to

bronze-tinted green by midsummer. The tree ultimately reaches about 25 feet tall and 20 feet wide.

PYRUS

PEAR

Zones vary. Full sun; regular water for fruiting types, moderate water for ornamentals. Deciduous.

Both the ornamental pears and the edible European type are fairly large, handsome trees that look good in all seasons. Early spring brings a froth of white blossoms about 1 inch across. As the flowers fade, glossy oval, 3-inch leaves emerge; these remain deep green during summer, then provide vivid color in fall. And in winter, the bare branch pattern makes a lovely display.

European pears, derived from *P. communis,* ultimately reach 30 to 40 feet high, 15 to 25 feet wide; they're pyramidal in shape, with strongly vertical branching. Choosing the right fruiting pear is a matter of matching each one's adaptability to your climate; consult your Cooperative Extension Office for advice on what's best for your region.

The most widely planted ornamental pears are *P. calleryana* and its selections, suited to Zones 2b–9, 14–21, 28, 31–41. Heights range from 30 to 50 feet, and shape varies considerably as well—pyramidal trees are most common, but columnar and rounded forms also exist. Ornamental pears bloom very early, before European ones; they produce very small, inedible fruits.

Pyrus calleryana

CHAPTER FIVE

SPECIALTY PLANTS TO COMPLETE THE PICTURE

Annuals, perennials, trees, shrubs, vines— each of these broad categories holds many excellent choices for the cottage garden, and you'll find a good selection discussed in the preceding chapter. But certain other plant groups merit special highlighting. In the next 22 pages, we offer descriptions of annual and perennial sorts of herbs; ornamental grasses; fruits and vegetables; and that most romantic of cottage garden components, the rose.

Roses, roses, roses... Since the mid-19th century, roses of all sorts—bush types and climbers, species and hybrids—have been an indispensable element of English-style cottage gardens. Shown here is the spring-flowering Rosa wichuraiana *hybrid 'Climbing American Beauty'.*

H E R B S

Wide and enormously varied, the world of herbs includes plants used for flavoring, those valued for their fragrance (be it attractive to humans or repellent to insects), and those once grown for medicinal or religious purposes but now planted largely for garden ornament. The following selection of favorite herbs—each attractive in leaf, in flower, or both—draws from all three categories.

Artemisia 'Powis Castle'

Foeniculum vulgare

ARTEMISIA

Perennials. Zones vary. Full sun; little to moderate water, except as noted.

Once used medicinally, the artemisias are valued today for the beauty of their foliage—finely divided, aromatic leaves in silvery gray, gray green, or soft green. With one exception, the flowers (in white, cream, or yellow) are tiny and scarcely noticeable. Most artemisias are woody-based, shrubby plants.

Angel hair, *A. schmidtiana* (Zones A1–A3, 1–10, 14–24, 29–45), with finely cut silvery white leaves, is a foreground plant to just 2 feet high and 1 foot wide. Its selection 'Silver Mound' is even smaller, reaching just 1 foot tall and broad.

Southernwood, *A. abrotanum* (Zones 2b–24, 27–41), forms a mound of feathery, lemon-scented gray-green leaves to 3 feet high and wide. Common wormwood, *A. absinthium* (Zones 2–24, 29–41), grows upright to 4 feet tall and 2 feet wide, its stems clothed in silvery gray, pungent foliage. Its presumed hybrid *A.* 'Powis Castle' (adapted to the same zones) is spreading rather than erect, eventually forming a 3-foot-tall, 6-foot-wide mound of lovely lacy, silvery leaves.

The sole artemisia to put on a significant flower show is white mugwort, *A. lactiflora* (Zones 1–9, 14–21, 29–43). Reaching as tall as 5 feet, the plant forms a 2-foot-wide clump of upright stems clothed in dark green, deeply lobed leaves; in late summer, showy branched sprays of small, creamy white flowers appear at the stem ends. Give this one moderate to regular water.

FOENICULUM vulgare

COMMON FENNEL

Perennial. Zones 2b–11, 14–24, 29–41, H1, H2. Full sun; moderate water. Self-sower.

Its leaves composed of multitudinous threadlike segments, a fennel plant looks something like a puff of green smoke in the landscape. Thick, pithy stems rise to around 5 feet tall, crowned during the summer months with broad, flat-topped clusters of small yellow flowers. Bronze fennel, *F. v.* 'Purpurascens' ('Smokey'), is identical save for foliage color—its leaves are a soft bronzy purple. In both kinds of fennel, the foliage turns brown in fall, then disintegrates, leaving bare stems and clustered seed heads. Both the fresh foliage and the seeds have a licorice flavor and can be used in cooking (bronze fennel leaves are typically used for garnishes). Fennel self-sows freely; if you don't gather the seeds, you may find yourself burdened next season with an overabundance of tenacious, tap-rooted volunteer plants.

HYSSOPUS officinalis

HYSSOP

Perennial. Zones 1–24, 30–45. Full sun or light shade; moderate to regular water. Self-sower.

A tidy-looking plant with a long bloom period, hyssop never registers as flashy—but it's eminently pleasant as a component of a mixed garden. Semiwoody stems outfitted in narrow, glossy leaves form a bushy, compact plant $1\frac{1}{2}$ to 2 feet high and 3 feet wide. From summer into fall, small flowers come in closely spaced whorls at the stem tips. The species bears blue-violet blossoms, but selections are available with flowers in white, pink, or lavender. The plant once had medicinal uses; the peppery, tangy leaves can be used in cooking.

LAVANDULA

LAVENDER

Evergreen shrubs. Zones vary. Full sun; moderate water. L stoechas is a self-sower.

Justly famous for their scent, the lavenders are equally esteemed for their ornamental value and ease of care. Plants vary in height from 1 foot to around 4 feet; narrow to needlelike leaves may be gray, gray green, or green. All bear fragrant flowers in congested spikes atop wire-thin stems; several species and hybrids bear especially sweet-scented blossoms that yield the lavender fragrance

so beloved in perfumes. The leaves, too, are aromatic and can impart a distinctive vinegary tang to certain foods.

The following three lavenders are the most widely adapted types, but gardeners in the West and Southwest have a number of additional choices (consult a knowledgeable local nursery or your Cooperative Extension Office for recommendations).

Spanish lavender, *L. stoechas* (Zones 4–24, 30, 31, warmer 32), ranges in height from $1\frac{1}{2}$ to 3 feet, depending on the selection. Leaves are gray green; distinctive spring flower spikes are chubby, square-cornered affairs, with small blackish maroon flowers and a four-petaled tuft of pinkish purple, rabbit ear–like bracts protruding from the top of each spike. This species self-sows profusely.

English lavender, *L. angustifolia* (Zones 2–24, 30, 32–34, 39), is the most widely grown species and the original source of lavender scent. It forms a 2- to $2\frac{1}{2}$-foot-high mound of gray leaves and bears lavender to violet summer flowers; selections include smaller plants and those in a wider range of blossom colors, including white and pink.

Summer-blooming lavandin or hedge lavender, *L. × intermedia*, grows in Zones 4–24, 30–34, 39. In general, it resembles a larger (to 4-foot-tall) *L. angustifolia*, though flower stems are branched and blossom spikes are looser. Named selections are shorter (2- to 3-foot) plants,

Hyssopus officinalis

Lavandula angustifolia

Nepeta × faassenii

Ocimum basilicum **'Dwarf Dark Opal'**

Origanum majorana

many with deep violet-blue blossoms; several of these are mainstays of the European lavender oil industry.

NEPETA

CATMINT

Perennials. Zones 1–24, 30, 32–43. Full sun; moderate water. Self-sowers.

An old-fashioned favorite for edging a pathway, billowy *N. × faassenii* (often sold as *N. mussinii*) forms a soft-looking mound about 1 foot high, up to 2 feet across. Small gray-green leaves are a backdrop for spikes of small blossoms that make a lavender-blue haze over the foliage from midspring into early summer. Taller, upright-growing species, reaching 2 to 3 feet, include *N. grandiflora,* with spikes of violet-blue blossoms in spring, and the similar *N. sibirica (N. macrantha),* bearing larger, darker flowers in summer.

OCIMUM basilicum

SWEET BASIL

Warm-season annual. All zones. Full sun; regular water. Self-sower.

Though it's native to tropical Asia, this easy-to-grow herb has become an essential flavoring in Mediterranean cuisine. Fast-growing, branching plants clothed in shiny, oval green leaves reach about 2 feet high and 1 foot wide; spikes of small white flowers appear at the stem tips, though these take energy from leaf production and should be pinched or cut out as soon as they appear. 'Dark Opal' and other selections with bronzy purple foliage are particularly effective for color contrast in mixed plantings. Basil is frost tender; sow seeds as soon as all danger of frost is past (or set out started plants at that time).

ORIGANUM

MARJORAM, OREGANO

Perennials. Zones vary. Full sun; little to moderate water.

The culinary marjorams and oreganos represent just a small part of this large and varied group. None is especially showy in flower, but all are attractive and useful.

Sweet marjoram, *O. majorana* (formerly classified as *Majorana hortensis*), is perennial in Zones 8–24, 29–31 and can be treated as a summer annual in colder regions. It grows in a clump to 2 feet high and wide, the branching stems outfitted in small, scoop-shaped light green leaves. In spring and summer, small white flowers appear at stem tips, nestled in knotlike, four-sided clusters of tiny leaves. Italian or Sicilian marjoram, *O. × majoricum* (Zones 4–24, 29–34), is similar but has slightly larger, more intensely flavored leaves.

Oregano, *O. vulgare,* grows in Zones 1–24, 30–45. Plants resemble those of *O. majorana,* but the dark green leaves are broader, flatter, and almost heart shaped; clumps can reach 2½ feet high and 3 feet wide, producing clusters of small white or purplish pink flowers from midsummer to early fall. Greek oregano, *O. v. hirtum* (Zones 8, 9, 12–24), is a variant of the species with especially pungent leaves.

PRUNELLA
HEAL-ALL, SELF-HEAL
Perennials. Zones 2–24, 29–43.
Full sun or light shade; regular
water. P. vulgaris *is a self-sower.*

As the common names suggest, these plants were once thought to be good for whatever ails you. Today, however, their efficacy is limited to garden decoration, where they indeed do an excellent job of forming dense, spreading, ground-hugging patches of oval to diamond-shaped leaves. In summer, somewhat leafy stems rise from the foliage, bearing elongated clusters of hooded flowers. *P. vulgaris* is the more common species, with purple or pink, $1/3$-inch blooms carried on 1-foot stems above a carpet of dark green, 2-inch leaves. *P. grandiflora* is larger in every way: it reaches $1^1/2$ feet high and has 4-inch leaves and 1- to $1^1/2$-inch flowers. The species bears purple blossoms, but selections offer purple-and-white, pink, and white flowers.

RUTA graveolens
RUE, HERB-OF-GRACE
Perennial. Zones 2–24, 30–41.
Full sun; moderate to regular water.

Pungently—even unpleasantly—aromatic foliage accounts for this plant's history of use as a medicine and disinfectant. In medieval times, it was also thought to protect against witchcraft, and brushes made of rue sprigs were once used in church services to sprinkle holy water.

In the garden, rue is a handsome, shrubby plant to 3 feet high and wide, with fernlike, finely divided bluish green leaves. In spring, clusters of yellowish green blossoms shaped like $1/2$-inch-wide single roses burst forth at the branch tips; these are followed by decorative brown seed capsules. Several named selections offer distinctly blue foliage on smaller-growing plants. For green leaves irregularly splashed in cream and yellow, look for 'Variegata'.

SANTOLINA chamaecyparissus
LAVENDER COTTON
Perennial. Zones 2–24, 27, 29, 30, 32–35, 39, H1, H2. Full sun; little to moderate water.

The strongly aromatic foliage explains this plant's former career as a medicine and insect repellent, but nowadays it is largely valued for beauty and an abuseproof constitution. It makes a frothy-looking, grayish white mound of very narrow, inch-long leaves, each finely divided into many feathery segments. Growth spreads horizontally—and indefinitely—by creeping, rooting stems; the branches arch upward to a foot or more. In late spring to early summer, the plant comes alive with brassy yellow

Prunella vulgaris

Ruta graveolens

Santolina chamaecyparissus

Teucrium chamaedrys

Thymus vulgaris

blooms—buttonlike, half-inch daisies without petals. 'Nana' and 'Pretty Carol' are lower growing, with a less spreading habit; 'Lemon Queen' has creamy yellow flowers.

TEUCRIUM chamaedrys
GERMANDER
Perennial. Zones 2–24, 28–41.
Full sun; moderate water.

This plant still plays one "culinary" role—as a flavoring for vermouth—but all of its ancient medical uses have faded into history. It now serves primarily as a handsome garden ornament, often used as a neat dark green border for beds of herbs in a classic knot garden. Oval leaves just shy of an inch long densely clothe spreading stems that reach about 1 foot high; in summer, spikes of reddish purple, $1/4$-inch flowers appear in loose spikes at the branch ends. Available selections include 'Prostratum', which spreads widely but reaches no higher than 6 inches, and a form with white flowers.

THYMUS
THYME
Perennials. Zones 1–24, 26,
28–43, except as noted. Full sun,
except as noted; moderate water.

We may think of thyme strictly as a culinary herb, but in the past it was used in perfumery, as a liqueur flavoring, and even in embalming. Many species and hybrids exist, offering quite an array of scents and flavors. Based on habit, the plants can be divided into two groups: bushy types and spreading ground covers. All prefer light shade in hot-summer regions.

Common thyme, *T. vulgaris,* is the classic culinary herb. It's a bushy plant to 1 foot high and 2 feet wide, with numerous wiry, branching stems sporting tiny, oval gray-green leaves. Tiny lilac-pink to white flowers appear at the stem tips in late spring and early summer. Silver thyme, *T. v.* 'Argenteus', has foliage variegated in silvery white.

Lemon thyme, *T. × citriodorus,* resembles its parent *T. vulgaris* but has slightly larger, lemon-scented leaves. Its named selections offer variety in foliage: 'Lime' has lime green leaves, while several others sport white or yellow variegation on a green background.

Creeping thyme or mother-of-thyme, *T. serpyllum* (formerly *T. praecox arcticus, T. drucei*), grows in Zones A2, A3, 1–24, 29–45. It forms a spreading, 3-inch-high mat of tiny, roundish dark green leaves; in summer, the foliage is spangled with purplish flowers. Creeping thyme is a favorite for planting between stepping-stones, where every footfall lightly crushes the leaves and releases a pleasant aroma. Specialists sell numerous named selections with various habits (some taller than the species, some smaller and more compact), finer-textured foliage, variations in scent, and blossoms in white, lavender, pink, or red. The leaves can be used in place of common thyme in cooking.

ORNAMENTAL GRASSES

Ornamental grasses are a contemporary addition to cottage gardens, but they fit right in: their stand-out shapes and feathery or spiky flower plumes offer yet one more way to bring variety to a planting. The size range is so wide that you'll find choices suitable for foreground, background, and in between; and in many, the flower stems are tall enough to serve as seasonal accents. Quite a few hold both foliage and blossoms throughout the winter, losing their charm only if battered by storms or crushed by snowfall.

The grasses below are classed as deciduous or evergreen. Be aware, though, that these terms have slightly different meanings when applied to grasses than they do when used to describe shrubs or trees. Evergreen grasses do maintain living foliage all year—but dead leaves must be removed as they become unsightly. Leaves of deciduous kinds die in fall or winter (though they may remain on the plants, often to decorative effect) and are replaced by fresh new foliage that rises from the ground the next year. For these types, cut back the previous year's dead growth before new leaves put on any significant size. (A few grasses are semievergreen: they maintain some degree of greenness during mild winters, but they should be cut back sharply before growth begins in spring.)

CALAMAGROSTIS × acutiflora

FEATHER REED GRASS

Zones 2b–24, 29–41. Full sun or partial shade; regular water.

Evergreen to semievergreen.

This grass forms tight clumps that make a distinctly vertical statement. Most widely sold is the selection 'Karl Foerster' ('Stricta'), with narrow, slightly arching, bright green leaves to about 3 feet high. In late spring or early summer, flower stalks rise to about 6 feet, bearing slender, feathery, purplish green plumes that age to buff; they remain attractive all through winter if not beaten down by storms.

DESCHAMPSIA cespitosa

TUFTED HAIR GRASS

Zones 2–24, 28–41. Partial shade, except as noted; regular water.

Evergreen.

One look at the foliage and you'll understand the common name "hair grass"—each clump of ultra-narrow, fountainlike leaves looks just like a mop of hair in need of a good combing. Clumps reach about 2 feet high and wide; in early summer, they send up arching, 3-foot stems bearing airy clouds of flowers that age from greenish gold to straw colored and persist into winter. Several named selections offer flowers in bronzy yellow or bright gold. Where summers are cool, hair grass enjoys a sunny location; elsewhere, give it partial shade.

FESTUCA

FESCUE

Zones vary. Full sun to light shade; moderate to regular water.

Evergreen.

The fescues are good candidates for startling pathway accents: at first glance, a passerby might almost think that an oversized blue or silver sea urchin has come to rest in the garden! The very narrow, wiry leaves form rounded mounds that reach 2 feet high and

Calamagrostis × acutiflora 'Karl Foerster'

Deschampsia cespitosa

Festuca glauca

Hakonechloa macra

Helictotrichon sempervirens

Imperata cylindrica

wide in the largest species and selections.

Common blue fescue, *F. glauca* (also sold as *F. ovina glauca* and *F. cinerea*), succeeds in Zones 1–24, 29–45; it's a foot-high mound of extra-fine, blue-gray to silvery white leaves. Flower stems rise above the foliage in summer, bearing upright, narrow spikes of blue blossoms that later turn buff. Named selections offer specific leaf colors; 'Siskiyou Blue', to 1 to 2 feet high, is a luminous blue.

Tufted fescue, *F. amethystina*, grows in Zones 2–10, 14–24, 29–43. Threadlike, blue-green to blue-gray leaves form a clump to 1½ feet high and wide; in late spring and early summer, stems tipped with arching, violet-tinted flower spikes reach 2 feet long. The selection 'Superba' has distinctly blue leaves and purple-tinted flower stems.

HAKONECHLOA macra
JAPANESE FOREST GRASS
Zones 2b–9, 14–24, 31–41. Partial shade, except as noted; regular water. Deciduous.

Think of this as a small, well-mannered bamboo. It spreads slowly by underground rhizomes, sending up slim, arching stems that bear narrow, dagger-shaped leaves to 10 inches long. Small flowers on lax stalks appear in early fall, but they're virtually lost amid the foliage. The gracefully mounding plant reaches 1½ to 2½ feet high, eventually expanding into a leafy drift. Selections with gold-striped or all-yellow foliage are the most widely sold. Where summers are very cool, Japanese forest grass will thrive in a sunny location; elsewhere, give it partial shade.

HELICTOTRICHON sempervirens (Avena sempervirens)
BLUE OAT GRASS
Zones 1–24, 30–41. Full sun; regular water. Evergreen to semievergreen.

Looking something like an oversize blue fescue *(Festuca glauca)*, blue oat grass forms a symmetrically rounded, blue-gray foliage fountain 2 to 3 feet high and wide. In late spring, the plant takes on the look of a burst of fireworks: needle-thin stems rise up to 2 feet above the narrow leaves, carrying wispy plumes of straw-colored flowers.

IMPERATA cylindrica 'Rubra' ('Red Baron')
JAPANESE BLOOD GRASS
Zones 2b–24, 26, 28, 31–43. Full sun or partial shade; regular water. Deciduous.

You can count on Japanese blood grass *not* to bloom—but when the foliage is this colorful, who needs flowers? Upright, flat new leaves rise from underground rhizomes each spring, reaching 1½ to 2 feet tall. Young leaves are green with red at their tips, but as the season progresses, the red color extends downward and intensifies, infusing at least half of each leaf blade. Clumps enlarge slowly as the rhizomes spread.

MISCANTHUS sinensis

EULALIA, JAPANESE SILVER GRASS

Zones 2–24, 29–41. Full sun or partial shade; moderate to regular water. Deciduous.

Fountains of narrow green leaves make a bulky yet graceful clump; stately blossom stems rise well above the leaves in summer or fall, bearing flower plumes in silvery to bronzy pink. In fall, the foliage turns to shades of yellow, orange, or bronze; it remains attractive during winter unless beaten down by storms. Many named selections are available, ranging from smaller kinds no taller than 3 feet to truly massive sorts that top out at 6 to 7 feet. You'll find a number of varieties with leaves variegated in yellow or white; these include choices with lengthwise stripes as well as some with horizontal banding.

MOLINIA caerulea

MOOR GRASS

Zones 1–9, 14–17, 32–41. Full sun or partial shade; regular water. Deciduous.

The various moor grasses are medium to large plants, but they don't look bulky—the clumps of narrow leaves and slender stems have a see-through quality. The species and its selections typically are fairly upright, light green clumps to 2 feet high and wide, with narrow, yellowish to purplish flower heads carried about 2 feet above the leaves. Selections of *M. c. arundinacea*, however, have broader gray-green leaves in clumps to 3 feet high, above which rise upright or gracefully arching flower stems that may reach 8 feet, depending on the selection. Leaves turn tawny yellow and dry out in fall, then detach (along with the flower stalks) from the plant's crown.

MUHLENBERGIA

Zones vary. Full sun or light shade; little to moderate water. Evergreen.

These tough but good-looking grasses are primarily native to the West, Southwest, Texas, and Mexico, where they have to cope with heat, wind, and drought. Bull grass, *M. emersleyi,* is the most widely adapted, growing in Zones 2–24, 30, 33, and 35. Glossy, almost threadlike green leaves grow in a mound to $1\frac{1}{2}$ feet high and 3 feet wide; in summer and fall, spikes of purplish flowers are carried 2 to 3 feet above the leaves.

Purple muhly, *M. rigida* (Zones 6–24, 30, 33), is another fairly low grower, forming a green mound to 2 feet high and wide; purple flowers come on 3-foot stems in late summer to fall. Pink muhly, *M. capillaris* (Zones 4–31), is a 3-foot-tall, 6-foot-wide haystack of leaves; feathery plumes of reddish fall flowers hover about 2 feet above the foliage.

The largest plant of the group is *M. lindheimeri* (Zones 6–24, 30, 33), a clump of arching blue-green leaves to 5 feet high and wide; in fall, arching spikes of amber flowers rise to around 7 feet.

Miscanthus sinensis **'Variegatus'**

Molinia caerulea **'Variegata'**

Muhlenbergia lindheimeri

Panicum virgatum

Pennisetum alopecuroides

Stipa gigantea

PANICUM virgatum
SWITCH GRASS
Zones 1–11, 14–23, 28–43.
Full sun or light shade; little to
regular water. Deciduous.

Native to the original high-grass
prairie, this impressive Mid-
westerner makes a thick, upright
clump of deep green to gray-
green leaves up to 4 feet high. In
summer, flowering stems topped
with loose clouds of pinkish blossoms rise as high as 3 feet above
the foliage. The leaves turn yellow
in fall, then soften to beige,
matching the faded flowers; leaves
and flowering stems persist over
winter. Among selected forms,
you'll find a few that offer red fall
color and several that are shorter
than the species.

Switch grass is highly adapt-
able in its moisture needs, thriving
with any amount of water.

PENNISETUM
FOUNTAIN GRASS
Zones vary. Full sun or partial
shade; moderate to regular water,
except as noted. Deciduous.

Their summer flowers really set
these grasses apart. Thick, elongated blossom clusters that look like
foxtails are held above the foliage
mass, carried at the tips of arching
stems. Oriental fountain grass,
P. orientale, grows in Zones 3–10,
14–24, 31–35, 37, 39. Its grayish
green leaves form a mound to 2
feet high and a bit wider, over-
topped by pinkish flower plumes
that mature to brown; leaves turn
straw colored in fall.

P. setaceum (Zones 8–24, 26,
27, warmer 28, 29, H1, H2) is a
dense green clump that can reach
5 feet in both directions; the
plumes of coppery pink and purple flowers are carried within
and just above the foliage. The
species is an invasive self-sower
that can crowd out native vegeta-
tion if planted near open areas,
but its form 'Rubrum' ('Cupre-
um'), with red-brown leaves and
pinkish flower plumes, usually
sets no seed. Leaves of the
species and its selections die back
in winter. Established plants are
very drought tolerant.

P. alopecuroides (Zones 2b–24,
31–35, 37, 39) is another large
fountain grass, forming clumps to
5 feet high and wide and flaunt-
ing pinkish flower plumes. The
bright green leaves turn yellow in
fall, then age to brown in winter.
Selected forms are shorter; one
of these, 'Little Bunny', tops out
at just 1½ feet.

STIPA gigantea
GIANT FEATHER GRASS
Zones 4–9, 14–24, 29–34, 39.
Full sun; moderate water. Evergreen.

Despite the name, this grass isn't
a giant for most of the year: it
forms a leafy green mass only
2 to 3 feet high and wide. The
impressive size comes in summer,
when stems shoot up to 6 feet
(and sometimes splay out to make
a clump that's just as wide), bearing airy clouds of yellowish flowers that sway in the breeze. Rising
from a mixed planting, they seem
to float in midair.

In today's garden, vegetables and small fruits are typically relegated to farm-style "efficiency" plots, with plants regimented in neat rows and blocks. But it doesn't have to be that way. Many edibles are ornamental enough to merit a place in the multihued tapestry of annuals, perennials, herbs, and shrubs that's a trademark of cottage gardening. And with edibles simply tucked in here and there—as they frequently were in the cottage gardens of old—you're less likely to be overwhelmed by the bumper crops that the modern (often overplanted) vegetable garden or berry patch tends to deliver.

ARTICHOKE

Perennial. Zones 4–9, 14–24, coastal 34 and 38. Full sun; regular water, except as noted.

Gardeners in Zones 8, 9, 14–24, and the coolest-summer parts of Zones 34 and 38 can raise artichokes for eating—but in all the zones noted above, the plants make strikingly ornamental additions to a mixed garden.

Each year, perennial roots send up a fountain of silvery green, deeply cut, 2½- to 3½-foot-long leaves, forming a plant about 4 feet high and up to 6 feet across. Sturdy flower stems rise above the foliage, producing large buds (the familiar globe artichokes) that open into 6-inch-wide, thistlelike blossoms of vivid blue purple. The flowers typically come in late spring and early summer, but in perpetually cool Zone 17, you'll get blossoms all year, with a harvest time that runs from September to May. In the other zones where crops are possible, you can harvest buds in early summer.

When grown strictly as ornamentals, artichokes will tolerate moderate to little watering in summer. If you're aiming for a crop, however, be sure to provide regular water.

ASPARAGUS

Perennial. Zones A1–A3, 1–24, 29–45. Full sun; regular water. Self-sower.

Asparagus has a growth cycle that makes it ideal for including in mixed plantings. Perennial roots send up new shoots in late winter or spring, depending on climate. You harvest these asparagus spears for a month or so, until new spears rising from the earth are no longer thick and succulent; then you let all subsequent shoots grow and mature. By mid- to late spring, you'll have a multistemmed plant bearing clouds of tiny leaves on countless branches.

A well-established asparagus clump will produce stems to about 6 feet high; positioned toward the back of a bed, it provides a wonderful green, feathery counterbalance to the varied flowers of spring and summer. In fall, leaves and stems turn tawny yellow and die back. Numerous named selections are available. All but those described as "all male" will produce a scattering of pea-size fruits that turn bright red when mature in summer (well before the leaves change color).

Artichoke

Asparagus

Scarlet runner bean 'Painted Lady'

Ornamental cabbage 'Osaka Red'

Chives

BEAN, HYACINTH and SCARLET RUNNER

Perennials grown as warm-season annuals. All zones. Full sun; regular water.

Why plant ordinary pole beans when you can grow these two and enjoy showy summer flowers as well as an edible crop? Both produce flat pods that can be harvested and eaten very young or gathered when mature for shelling out.

Hyacinth bean, *Dolichos lablab (Lablab purpureus),* is a fast-growing, twining plant to 10 feet high, covered in leaves made up of three broadly oval leaflets. Showy long-stemmed, loose clusters of sweet pea–shaped purple (or purple-and-white) flowers are followed by velvety pods in a brilliant magenta purple.

Scarlet runner bean, *Phaseolus coccineus,* has bright green leaves that resemble those of hyacinth bean in shape and size, but the plant itself is larger, climbing to 20 feet and capable of blanketing fences, arbors, and sheds. Sweet pea–shaped, vivid scarlet blossoms appear in elongated, slender clusters; the pods that follow the flowers are dark green. 'Painted Lady', with white-and-red blooms, is also available.

CABBAGE and KALE, FLOWERING

Cool-season annuals. All zones. Full sun; regular water.

While a typical head of cabbage or kale may be better eaten than admired, these ornamental strains are real show-offs—edible, yes, but almost too pretty to harvest. Plants form 10-inch-wide rosettes of curly leaves that resemble giant, earthbound, deep blue-green peonies strikingly marbled and edged in white, cream, rose, or purple. Flowering kale forms a slightly looser head than flowering cabbage and has more heavily fringed leaf margins, but otherwise the two are virtually identical.

Planting time depends on climate. Where winters are cold and snowy and summers relatively cool, set out plants in spring, 4 to 6 weeks before the last-frost date; they'll mature in summer and last into the fall. In cold-winter regions with hot summers, follow the same schedule but plant on the early side, so that heads will mature before heat puts a stop to growth.

In milder-winter regions (featuring frosts and freezes, but usually no snow), set out plants in fall; in desert areas with very mild winters and hot summers, plant in late summer and fall. In both these regions, you'll get a display of mature heads in winter and early spring.

CHIVES

Perennial. All zones. Full sun or partial shade; regular water. Self-sower.

Not quite vegetable, not quite herb, this onion-family member is a favorite garnish for a number of dishes. An individual plant looks like a petite, plain scallion—but a cluster of chives is ornamental indeed, a fountainlike clump of grassy, tubular leaves bursting with cloverlike heads of pink, violet-scented blossoms during spring. Especially well-grown clumps can reach 2 feet high, but 1 to 1½ feet is a more typical size.

EGGPLANT

Warm-season annual. All zones.
Full sun; regular water.

Glossy-skinned eggplants are as handsome in the garden as they are in the produce market. Plants grow 2 to 3 feet high and wide, sporting large, lobed leaves and pendent, star-shaped, violet flowers about 1½ inches across all summer long. The standard eggplant is an oblong, bronzy purple fruit up to a foot long, but there are other shapes, sizes, and colors as well: standard-size fruits in white; smaller, round or oval ones in white, yellow, red, or green; and long, slender Japanese types in purple, lavender, or white. Most eggplants need a long (2- to 3-month) growing season in order to ripen a crop; in short-summer regions, plant only fast-maturing varieties. Set out plants as soon as daytime temperatures reach 70°F/21°C.

PEACH, GENETIC DWARF

Deciduous shrub. Zones vary.
Full sun; regular water.

Ordinary peach trees have a brief moment of beauty during their springtime bloom—after which you're left waiting for fruit to ripen on a plant of no particular charm. You're likely to need a ladder to reach all the fruits, and the trees need annual pruning if they're to produce well. Genetic dwarf peaches, on the other hand, give you lovely flowers and delicious fruit on shrubby, long-leafed plants with a shaggy, sheepdog-like appeal. Their small stature—they reach just 5 to 6 feet tall and wide—means the crop is easy to pick. The plants don't require pruning to stay productive; you need trim them only for shape.

Available selections vary in climate preference. Some take the cold winters of Zones 2 and 39 but won't perform in mild-winter areas, while others will fruit where winter cold is minimal. For information on the varieties best suited to your area, check with your Cooperative Extension Office or a reputable local nursery.

PEPPER

Warm-season annuals. All zones.
Full sun; regular water.

Beyond the familiar green, yellow, and red bells, there's an entire universe of sweet to hot peppers in numerous shapes, sizes, and colors. All are attractive, bushy plants clothed in shiny, oval green leaves; depending on the kind of pepper, plant height ranges from 1 foot to 5 feet, leaf size from 1 to 4 inches long. Sweet peppers (exemplified by the bell type) are typically short-

Eggplant

Genetic dwarf peach 'Southern Sweet'

Pepper

Rhubarb

Strawberry

er plants with larger leaves, while hot types are taller, more spreading plants with smaller foliage. All peppers are frost tender, so wait to plant them until after the last frost, when daytime temperatures have reached 65°F/18°C. Harvest will start in 2 to 3 months, with hot peppers generally requiring the longer time to come into production. Plants cease bearing during stretches of intensely hot weather, then resume production as weather cools toward fall.

RHUBARB

Perennial. Zones A1–A3, 1–11, 14–24, 26–45. Full sun, except as noted; regular water.

Even if it didn't produce edible leafstalks, rhubarb would be worth growing: a thriving clump is a handsome foliage plant, a leafy mound 3 feet high and 4 to 5 feet across. The dark green, heavily textured, broadly arrow-shaped leaves are up to 1½ feet long and 1 foot wide, each carried at the end of a thick leafstalk to 1½ feet long. Varieties with rosy red to dark red leafstalks are most common, but green-stalked kinds also are grown; the flavor is the same regardless of color. Flowers are insignificant and draw energy from leaf production, so cut out blossom stems as they appear.

By nature, this perennial is a cold-winter/cool-summer plant that needs at least a bit of winter chill to produce the thickest leafstalks—but tolerable crops are

possible even where winters are mild. In hot-summer regions, locate plants in partial shade.

STRAWBERRY

Perennials. Zones A1–A3, 1–9, 14–24, 26–45, H1, H2. Full sun; regular water.

Sweet, tempting strawberries are the perfect cottage garden component. Tuck a few plants in here and there along a pathway, where you can enjoy the beauty of their low-growing foliage and easily pluck the shiny fruits as they ripen. Each leaf consists of three oval, toothed, long-stalked leaflets; plants form foliage clumps to about 8 inches high and extend their territory by sending out rooting runners that give rise to new plants. Clusters of white flowers that resemble tiny (½- to 1-inch) single roses appear in clusters on long individual stalks.

Two general types of strawberries are sold. June-bearing kinds begin fruiting at some point in spring and produce berries into the summer; everbearing varieties also start to bear in spring, but they continue on into fall, hitting their peak in summer. June-bearing strawberries generally produce heavier crops of better-tasting berries than everbearing sorts do. Countless named varieties exist, developed not only for fruit quality but also for different climates. Consult your Cooperative Extension Office for advice on the best choices for your area.

SUNFLOWER

Warm-season annual. All zones.
Full sun; regular water.

Big, brash sunflower blossoms are the epitome of high summer. Virtually no plant is easier to grow—and few give you so much bounty from a single seed. Varieties grown for seed production are a special breed of the common sunflower, *Helianthus annuus.* Most of them make giant, single-stemmed plants that rise 10 feet or higher, bearing large leaves with a broad arrow shape. Atop the single stem comes a solitary flower up to a foot in diameter—a broad, dark brown central disk surrounded by one ring of yellow petals. A few shorter selections have been developed; one choice is 'Sunspot', with a 10-inch blossom on a 2- to 3-foot stem. Plant sunflower seeds about 4 weeks after the last frost, when weather is sure to stay warm. Plants grow quickly; heads will be ready for harvest about 80 days after sowing.

SWISS CHARD

Biennial grown as annual. All zones.
Full sun; regular water.

When you grow Swiss chard, you really can have your cake and eat it too. Individual outer leaves will be ready to harvest within about 2 months after planting, and new leaves will continue to grow from the plant's center for months, giving you an ongoing crop. The plant resembles an exotic lettuce: leafstalks arise from one point,

each topped with an upright, elongated, puckery-textured leaf with a thickened midrib. A number of varieties are sold, typically reaching 1 to 1½ feet high; selections with colored leafstalks, such as 'Rhubarb' and 'Bright Lights', are especially decorative. Though it's a cool-season biennial, Swiss chard remains healthy even through hot summers, but the leaves take on a rather bitter flavor in steamy weather.

In cold-winter regions, sow seeds in early spring, as soon as soil is workable; you'll be able to harvest leaves from late spring until frost. In mild-winter areas with snowless winters, sow seeds from winter to early spring for spring-through-fall harvest; or sow in late summer to early fall for harvest beginning in winter.

ZUCCHINI

Warm-season annual. All zones.
Full sun; regular water.

That's right: the ubiquitous giveaway vegetable comes on an attractive plant! The original zucchini plants were sprawling vines, but you can now buy bush types that simply form hefty clumps. Plants grow 2 to 4 feet high and wide and look a bit like rough-textured rhubarb, with big, wavy-edged leaves at the ends of long leafstalks. Large, funnel-shaped yellow flowers precede the green or yellow fruits, which vary in shape from long and slender to almost spherical. Plant seeds in spring, after frost danger is past.

Sunflower

Swiss chard 'Bright Lights'

Zucchini

R O S E S

Think of an English village, and you're bound to include a rose-festooned cottage or two in the picture. And that's as it should be. As the cottage garden style became more defined in the 19th and early 20th centuries, roses were given a place of prominence—and their popularity hasn't waned with the years. Today's cottage gardener can select from a vast array of roses, including many of the best from past centuries. On these eight pages, we offer an overview of good choices, touching first on climbers, then going on to bush types. Within each of these groups, you'll find spring-flowering roses—those that mount just one lavish show in spring, then put on growth for the following year—as well as repeat bloomers, which give you several waves of blossoms from spring until frost.

Most roses will need some amount of winter protection where temperatures regularly dip to 5° F/ − 15° C or lower. Certain varieties and groups survive much colder conditions, however, while others are more tender—and for these, we indicate specific hardiness limits or suitable climate zones.

In the discussion that follows, we describe flower sizes as small (less than 1½ inches across), medium (1½ to 3 inches), or large (over 3 inches). For more detailed descriptions of many rose varieties and information on planting and care, refer to Sunset's Roses.

CLIMBING ROSES

Roses that can cover the sides of cottages, frame windows, drape over doorways—all these plants are lumped together as "climbing roses." In truth, they don't really climb the way twining vines or those with coiling tendrils do; they have only thorns with which to hook their pliable canes into place. They can scramble on their own through shrubbery and trees, but if you're growing them on structures, you'll need to tie them in place (at least initially). Aside from the hardiest Canada-bred types, which will survive winters unprotected in zones as cold as 1 and 43, all climbers need some protection where temperatures routinely fall to 10°F/–12°C or below.

SPRING-FLOWERING CLIMBERS

Including species roses as well as hybrids, this group offers plenty of choices. Plant size ranges from fairly modest to frankly huge; flower form and color vary widely, too.

Species roses

In Zones 4–33, H1, H2, Lady Banks' rose, *R. banksiae,* is unsurpassed for its stunning spring display. The super-vigorous plant is a prime candidate for arbors and pergolas (and the walls of two-story houses), where the long, slender, thornless canes can develop unrestricted. The most common form is 'Lutea', bearing clusters of small, unscented, double yellow blossoms; violet-scented 'Alba Plena' is its white counterpart. Cherokee rose, *R. laevigata* (Zones 4–9, 14–31, warmer 32, H1, H2), is a thorny, rampant climber suitable for the same uses as *R. banksiae.* Impressive large, single white flowers are displayed against lustrous dark green leaves.

Hybrid roses

Though repeat bloomers are by far the most widely sold hybrid

Rosa banksiae (spring climber)

'Mme. Grégoire Staechelin' (spring climber)

'Alchymist' (spring climber)

climbers, you'll still find some spring-flowering kinds—including the following, unequalled for beauty and charm. 'Alchymist' is a restrained grower (to about 12 feet) producing large, packed-with-petals blossoms that mingle apricot, gold, orange, and pink. 'Mme. Grégoire Staechelin' offers big, sumptuous, hybrid tea–style ruffled pink blossoms on a husky, 20-foot plant. Old favorite 'Paul's Scarlet Climber' reaches about 12 feet and dazzles with a mass display of clustered medium-size flowers in unfading crimson. The wichuraiana ramblers, derived from crosses of *R. wichuraiana* with tea or hybrid tea roses, produce bountiful clusters of medium-size blooms on strong-growing plants that typically have limber canes and glossy foliage. Coral pink 'Albertine', creamy white 'Albéric Barbier', buff yellow 'Gardenia', and cerise 'Climbing American Beauty' are good representatives.

REPEAT-FLOWERING CLIMBERS

The roses in this class include both old types—dating as far back as the mid-1800s—and modern hybrids.

Old roses

In mild-winter Zones 6–9, 12–31, warmer 32, H1, H2, gardeners can enjoy two groups of free-blooming but fairly tender old climbers. *Noisette* roses, named for the man who helped develop them, feature modest clusters of small to large flowers (depending on the variety) on well-foliaged plants in a range of sizes. *Climbing tea* roses are vigorous growers with large blossoms which, in some varieties, look just like those of modern hybrid teas. In both groups, the prevailing colors are delicate and subtle—cream, white, and soft shades of yellow, pink, and orange. Favorite Noisettes still available today include white 'Aimée Vibert Scandens' and 'Lamarque'; yellow 'Alister Stella Gray' and 'Maréchal Niel'; and apricot to orange blends 'Jaune Desprez' and 'Rêve d'Or'. Among teas, old favorites are pink 'Climbing Maman Cochet' and its white form 'White Climbing Maman Cochet', and soft apricot orange 'Gloire de Dijon'.

Two other 19th-century hybrids (from other rose classes) are also widely grown in the mild-winter zones. 'Climbing Cécile Brunner' can reach 20

'Albéric Barbier' (spring climber)

'Albertine' (spring climber)

'Climbing Cécile Brunner' (repeat climber)

'Gloire de Dijon' (repeat climber)

'Alister Stella Gray' (repeat climber)

feet, bearing clusters of small, pink hybrid tea–like buds that open to loose, soft-looking blossoms. Thornless 'Zéphirine Drouhin' produces medium-size, semidouble cerise blossoms on a more restrained plant that climbs to about 12 feet.

Modern roses

The most widely sold modern climbers bear flowers in the hybrid tea mold, with shapely buds opening to large, full blossoms. Some of these are natural climbers, while others are climbing sports (natural mutations) of bush roses. Floral beauty is their strong point, since many (especially the hybrid tea sports) are rather stiff plants that have no special appeal when out of flower. Before making a choice, try to see an established plant in bloom.

For extra-hardy climbers, look to the Canadian Explorer series, developed to endure southern Canadian winters with little or no protection. These are plants of modest stature that also can be grown as large shrubs; the semidouble to double, medium-size blossoms usually come in clusters. Examples include red 'Henry Kelsey' and 'John Cabot' and carmine pink 'William Baffin'.

Several distinctive modern climbers rate special mention. 'Altissimo', reaching about 10 feet, is a somewhat stiff, shrubby plant with small clusters of large single blossoms in velvety scarlet. 'Blaze', a child of long-time favorite 'Paul's Scarlet Climber', offers clusters of medium-size, loose-looking blooms on a truly climbing plant of modest size (12 to 15 feet). The floribunda

'Climbing Iceberg' is unsurpassed among whites, bearing medium-size hybrid tea–like blossoms on a vigorous grower to about 15 feet. 'Mermaid' is suited just to Zones 7–28, where it can become a massive, thorny, glossy-leafed plant spangled with large single yellow blossoms from spring until frost. 'New Dawn', a 15-footer with shiny dark green foliage, bears medium-size, semidouble hybrid tea–style flowers in a luscious soft, silvery pink; its sport 'Awakening' differs only in having ultra-double flowers that open flat, looking more like old centifolia or damask roses.

BUSH ROSES

In the mixed garden, roses are second to no other flowering shrubs. The choices are extensive. You'll find many old European

'John Cabot' (repeat climber)

'Altissimo' (repeat climber)

Rosa roxburghii (spring bush)

'New Dawn' (repeat climber)

'Celestial' (alba)

sorts—which would certainly have been among the first roses to be included in cottage gardens—as well as a long, long list of modern selections in a dazzling color array. Among modern sorts, current breeding programs are greatly expanding the catch-all category "shrub roses"—plants designed not to provide perfect long-stemmed blooms for cutting, but to serve as basic, relatively low-maintenance flowering shrubbery.

As is true for climbing types, bush roses include both spring- and repeat-flowering plants.

SPRING-FLOWERING BUSH ROSES

Most rose species and their hybrids are valued for lavish floral displays in spring. The hybrids in this group—the well-loved old European roses—bloom somewhat less profusely than the species, but their blossoms are generally larger and more complex in appearance.

Species roses

These lovely wild roses offer a varied assortment of worthwhile individuals. Austrian brier, *R. foetida* (Zones A2, A3, 1–21, 32–41), is best known through its form 'Bicolor' ('Austrian Copper'), with medium-size single blooms composed of two-color petals—orange on the upper surface, yellow on the underside. The plant reaches 5 feet high and wide. Another *R. foetida* variant is 'Persiana' ('Persian Yellow'), with double yellow blooms. The *R. foetida* hybrid 'Harison's Yellow' (Zones 1–24, 30–45) is an upright 6-footer with fine-textured foliage and semidouble yellow flowers.

Forming a rounded, 6-foot bush with almost fernlike foliage and decorative peeling bark, chestnut rose (*R. roxburghii*) succeeds in Zones 2–24, 26–41. Prickly buds that look like chestnut burrs open to medium-size, lilac-pink double flowers ('Normalis' has single blooms).

Father Hugo's rose, *R. xanthina hugonis* (Zones 2–24, 32–41), is an upright-arching, 8-foot bush; small, bright yellow single flowers transform it into a golden fountain in spring.

Requiring plenty of space, *R. moyesii* (Zones 3–10, 14–21, 32–34, 39) grows to an open-structured bush, 10 feet high and wide. Medium-size single blossoms in a striking bright red are followed by bottle-shaped scarlet hips.

Rosa foetida 'Bicolor' (spring bush)

'Superb Tuscan' (gallica)

'Apothecary's Rose' (gallica)

'Cabbage Rose' (centifolia)

Old roses

These venerable hybrid classes were all developed in Europe prior to the introduction of repeat-flowering roses from Asia. They embrace a variety of plant types; the blossoms vary in form as well, but all are typically medium to large, in colors ranging from white through pink shades to red and violet.

Alba roses are large, upright plants with handsome grayish green leaves; pleasantly scented, single to very double flowers come in white and delicate pink shades. 'Alba Maxima' and 'Alba Semi-plena' are good white individuals; choice pinks include 'Celestial', 'Félicité Parmentier', 'Great Maiden's Blush', and 'Königin von Dänemark'.

Centifolia roses derive their name from their packed-with-petals flowers. Coming in pink, white, and violet, the heavily perfumed blossoms are borne on plants that often reach 5 to 6 feet, with lax canes that tend to arch or sprawl from the weight of the flowers. 'Blanchefleur' and 'Unique Blanche' are white representatives; 'Cabbage Rose' and 'Paul Ricault' are rich pink.

Intensely fragrant *damask* roses are typically arching, thorny 5-foot bushes. The blooms are pink or white; in many varieties, they are circular, flat, and full of countless small petals. Soft pink 'Celsiana', deep pink 'Marie Louise', and elegant white 'Mme. Hardy' are choice examples.

Gallica roses offer the color red in all its variations—from pink to deep violet red—in semidouble to extremely double blooms that are usually fragrant.

Plants reach 4 to 5 feet high; they're upright growers lacking the more relaxed demeanor of albas, centifolias, and damasks. 'Tuscany' and 'Superb Tuscan' are darkest, velvety red; 'Charles de Mills' bears crimson blooms with tints of purple, lavender, and pink. Historic 'Apothecary's Rose' (*R. gallica* 'Officinalis') has semidouble cherry red blossoms; its sport 'Rosa Mundi' (*R. gallica* 'Versicolor') shows irregular pink and red dashes and flecks on a white background.

Moss roses are variants of centifolia and damask roses in which the green calyx (the sheath from which the flower emerges) is encrusted in decorative green glands that give it a mossy look. In other respects, the plants are like any other member of their class. Colors include white, red,

'Mme. Hardy' (damask)

'Paul Ricault' (centifolia)

'White Bath' (moss)

pink, and purple. The original pink moss rose, 'Communis', is a typical pink centifolia with moss added; its sport 'White Bath' is identical save for its white blooms. 'William Lobb', another centifolia moss, features striking semidouble blossoms in a rich mix of magenta, crimson, purple, and lavender. Damask mosses include full-petaled, pale pink 'Comtesse de Murinais' and semidouble red 'Henri Martin'.

REPEAT-FLOWERING BUSH ROSES

Most repeat-blooming bush roses are modern hybrids, but you'll also find some worthy old roses in the group.

Old roses

Unlike the old European kinds, China and tea roses give you more than a springtime show: where winter temperatures reliably remain above 10°F/−12°C (roughly Zones 6–9, 12–31, H1, H2), they'll provide wave after wave of bloom throughout the growing season. *Chinas* are smaller than teas, generally growing 2 to 4 feet high and bearing small clusters of medium-size flowers. White 'Ducher', rose pink 'Old Blush' ('Parson's Pink China'), and velvety bright red 'Cramoisi Supérieur' ('Agrippina') are among the best.

Tea roses are the precursors of modern hybrid teas and resemble them in flower form; many have long, pointed buds that scroll open to large, full blossoms. The plants grow 3 to 6 feet high (even taller, in some cases). Among the many superb choices are semidouble apricot buff 'Safrano' and saffron yellow 'Lady Hillingdon', both with bronzy purple new growth; ultravigorous 'Mons. Tillier', bearing flat, very full blossoms in a mix of soft brick and carmine red; and 'Duchesse de Brabant', with tulip-shaped blooms in a soft, warm pink. Those with flowers most like hybrid teas include deep pink 'Mme. Lambard'; creamy pink 'Maman Cochet' and its pink-tinted white sport 'White Maman Cochet'; and 'Mrs. Dudley Cross' and 'Marie van Houtte', both with yellow-and-cream blooms tinged in pink.

Modern roses

This huge category includes a wide range of hybrid groups, each including named selections in bewildering variety. Good choices for cottage gardens include the

'Cramoisi Supérieur' (China)

'Mons. Tillier' (tea)

'Maman Cochet' (tea)

'Simplicity' (floribunda)

'Iceberg' (floribunda)

highly developed classes of floribundas and miniature roses, as well as the more heterogeneous group labeled "shrub roses." The enormously popular hybrid tea roses, however, are less successful in cottage gardens. Mass marketed in catalogs and nurseries, these roses were developed for beauty of individual flowers (often borne on long stems for cutting); they are fairly stiff plants that don't bloom as lavishly as the other recommended types. Moreover, they require regular attention to fertilizing and pest control for the best performance.

Floribundas and miniatures

Originally developed to function as fairly low-growing flowering shrubs, floribunda roses bear clusters of small to medium-size blooms. The original floribundas had an informal wild rose charm, but breeders have worked to create flowers with more refined (hybrid tea–like) form, in a vast color range. Varieties are numerous, and availability changes constantly. Classics include red 'Europeana', pink 'Simplicity' and 'Betty Prior', creamy white 'French Lace', pure white 'Iceberg', and yellow 'Sun Flare'.

Miniature roses have undergone frenzied development in the last 50 years. The result is a diverse assortment offering all the colors and color patterns found in modern hybrid teas— and in fact, many minis simply look like small versions of their larger kin. Flower size varies from about 1 inch to nearly 3 inches across. The plants all stay relatively small when container grown, but when they're set into the ground, size can vary greatly; some become dense, twiggy plants up to 4 feet tall. New varieties appear regularly, pushing older ones out of general circulation. Among those of enduring quality are orange-red 'Starina', pink 'Millie Walters', pink blends 'Jean Kenneally' and 'Minnie Pearl', white 'Gourmet Popcorn', red-and-white 'Magic Carrousel', yellow 'Rise 'n' Shine', and red-edged yellow 'Rainbow's End'.

Give both floribundas and miniatures winter protection where temperatures regularly fall to 10°F/−12°C or lower.

Shrub roses

This category is so diverse that generalizations are impossible—but it can, nonetheless, be loosely separated into several groups. When it comes time to choose a specific variety,

'Magic Carrousel' (miniature)

'Gourmet Popcorn' (miniature)

'Abraham Darby' (shrub)

'Mary Rose' (shrub)

consult up-to-date rose books and catalogs, and try your best to see the plant actually growing in a garden.

Hybrid musk roses are a small group of early 20th-century hybrids with clusters of small to medium-size flowers borne on plants that can be kept shrubby or, in most varieties, trained as small climbers. Most thrive in partial shade. Coppery apricot 'Cornelia', pink 'Felicia', and salmon coral 'Penelope' are favorites.

Hardy hybrid roses are the result of Midwestern and Canadian breeding programs aimed at producing plants able to survive prairie and northern winters without protection (they can even take the cold of Zones 1 and 43). The Midwestern hybrids, such as 'Country Dancer' and 'Prairie Princess', resemble large floribundas or hybrid teas; the Canadian group—many named for Canadian explorers ('Martin Frobisher', for example)—make larger bushes with loose, informal flowers.

Trademarked rose groups represent a recent trend in marketing: individual named roses are promoted as members of what are essentially brand-name family groups. All are worth consideration, since they have been developed with beauty *and* ease of maintenance in mind. The trend-setters were the David Austin English Roses, hybrids that merge the floral style of old European roses with the colors and repeat-flowering habit of modern hybrid teas ('Mary Rose' and 'Abraham Darby' are examples). Later introductions include the Romantica, Generosa, and Renaissance roses, all represented by growing numbers of named individuals. Also in this group are the Meidiland roses, marvelous for mass effect—mounding, medium to large shrubs with small flowers in large clusters. 'Scarlet Meidiland' and 'White Meidiland' are just two of the many choices.

Miscellaneous shrub roses form a catch-all category—a repository for repeat-flowering, shrubby roses that don't fit any of the shrub groups just described. Noteworthy varieties include rose pink 'Bonica', white 'Sea Foam', pink-and-white 'Carefree Wonder', and 'Sally Holmes', which can grow as a shrub or a climber and bears clusters of single pinkish white flowers reminiscent of apple blossoms.

'Sea Foam' (shrub)

'Sally Holmes' (shrub)

'Felicia' (shrub)

'Penelope' (shrub)

CHAPTER SIX

DETAILS 🌿
AND
ACCESSORIES

Plants and flowers make a cottage garden—you can't really have one without them!—but various other components also contribute charm and distinction. Among these are framework items: the pathway in its many variations, "dividers" such as fences and hedges, and gates. Structural details comprise other typically permanent features, including tripods, arches, arbors, and trellises. Finally, garden accessories run from useful items such as benches, containers, sundials, and bird feeders to strictly decorative pieces of garden art.

Brimming with an exuberant assortment of cottage garden classics, this sunny back garden has color aplenty…and more is on the way, thanks to the strategically placed ceramic birdbath and hanging feeder, two irresistible lures for feathered visitors.

A sinuous gravel path ultimately wends its way to a weathered barn, but the indirect route slows your walking pace to a stroll, inviting you to savor the garden's scents and colors as you pass by. Framing this Pacific Northwest planting is a flowering dogwood in full cry.

Details and accessories are all about style, about expressing the cottage garden spirit in your own way. Whether you favor a rustic, traditional look or a slightly more polished one, you can choose paths and fences, benches and bird houses that suit you—and the garden—perfectly.

PATHWAYS

The garden path is more than a conduit from here to there. It's a way to say "welcome—please come inside." As you work to create this hospitable mood, you'll want to think about the path's size, its shape, and the materials it's made from. As far as size goes, keep in mind that really wide paths tend to look like driveways or two-way jogging trails. A narrower path will lend the cozier, more intimate feel you're after—just don't make it so narrow that guests can't walk side by side without being crowded or engulfed by bordering plants.

Shape, too, influences the garden's atmosphere. In the earliest cottage gardens, the main pathway ran straight from street to front door. Today, however, it may be straight, sinuous, or angled—and it may not even end up at the house. If you take the straight-arrow approach, with a clear destination in plain view, you'll achieve a more open feeling, letting guests enjoy the whole garden all at once. Add curves and angles, though, and you add some mystery: a walk along the path can be a journey of discovery, with something unexpected—a rose arbor, a sundial surrounded with fragrant herbs—around each bend.

The material used to make a pathway is important, too. The original choice was compacted earth—simple, but a mess in wet weather. The better paths, though, were created from durable indigenous materials such as fieldstone, slate, or pebbles. These same materials were often used to build the cottage itself, making dwelling and garden seem all of a piece, as if they'd simply grown naturally from the site. Using native or

Leading through a Southern California contemporary cottage garden, a crazy-paving pathway draws you to a weathered bench, a comfy spot for relaxation and contemplation. Designed for the region's Mediterranean climate, the planting features sun-loving, less-thirsty plants.

regional materials for pathways is still a fine idea today.

One popular choice is gravel —attractive, relatively inexpensive, and easy to install. Be aware, though, that gravel tends to "migrate," moving from the center of the path (the most heavily trafficked area) to the margins, and even into the edges of planting beds. Gravel is often also used as filler between larger permanent path components like stone or wood rounds.

Strictly for strolling, this path of unmortared flagstones ascends a gradual slope and ends at a simple birdbath. Spaces between the stones leave room for low-growing annuals and perennials.

If you like the look of bare earth but don't want to deal with mud and dust, consider using rock crushed to an almost sandy consistency; decomposed granite and blue shale are two familiar examples, though choices vary from region to region. All these materials pack firmly, making a clean, natural-looking surface for walking.

Even if there's no suitable native material, you can still link home and garden by making pathways from materials used in your home's construction—brick paving with a brick house, for example, or wood rounds or rough timbers embedded in gravel to match a home built of natural wood. (Wood chips also make good-looking paths, but they eventually decompose, so be aware that you'll need to replenish them periodically.) If you cannot achieve a close match, simply aim for a suitably rustic-looking pathway that harmonizes with the building materials nearby. Avoid anything overly formal (herringbone brick, for example) or clinically hard (such as smooth poured concrete).

Turf grass isn't part of the cottage garden tradition, but it can still serve quite well as a countrified green ribbon cutting through billowing floral plantings. Just heed two important pointers. First, limit the width to good strolling size; anything broader looks like lawn bordered by flower beds. Second, be sure the turf pathway looks casual; don't manicure it to golf course standards.

The best cottage garden fences create boundaries, not barriers. These simple pickets do form a physical separation, but they also allow you to see through and over. The open structure permits good air circulation in the beds on either side—a must for keeping plants healthy.

FENCES, WALLS, AND HEDGES

Not all cottage gardens feature definite boundaries, but if you do opt to enclose your planting (or to have it abut a barrier such as a fence or hedge), make sure the boundary's size, bulk, and material suit the cottage style.

The original cottage garden enclosures were made from local materials: stone, wood, or hedge plants. They tended to be of modest height—tall enough to keep out wandering livestock, but not so high as to loom over the surroundings. Even today, the most true-to-mood cottage gardens are bounded by relatively low fencing; the plants growing nearby can tumble over it at will, allowing passersby outside the fence to enjoy the garden's scents and colors.

FENCES Wood is the material of choice; it has the mellow, natural look that complements the traditional tousled plantings. You'll find enormous variety in manufactured lumber, both in kinds of wood and in board dimensions. A basic flat plank fence is

LEFT *Rustic post-and-rail construction produces the ultimate see-through fencing—and lets plants blur the garden's boundaries by growing through and around the railings.* **RIGHT** *At the other end of the density scale is a thick-foliaged hedge trimmed into a wide archway over a stone path, here serving both as a boundary and as a transition to another part of the garden.*

the simplest style, but it doesn't have to be boring; you can work wonders by varying the size and spacing of the planks. The time-honored picket fence falls into this category. It can be made with rustic, unfinished boards or, at the fancier end of the scale, from painted pickets with decoratively carved tops. For a cottage garden, simpler is better, and coordinating fence with house may answer the weathered versus painted question.

If you prefer a very open look, you can opt for a post-and-rail framework alone, sans planks. Such a fence effectively marks boundaries while still allowing a clear view of the garden on the other side. Post-and-rail can be executed with precisely dimensioned lumber or, for a more rustic mood, with peeled-trunk posts and hand-hewn crosspieces.

WALLS Stone is the world's oldest wall material: the dry stone fences of Great Britain and New England are classic examples. Rising from a broad, firm base and often partially covered with moss and lichen, such fences look entirely wedded to the site. To enhance the illusion of a naturally occurring structure, stack the stones without mortar—or, if mortar is essential for stability, use it as inconspicuously as possible. For cottage gardens, irregular stones are preferable to carefully dressed blocks, which tend to look factory made.

Concrete and brick, the two other widely available wall materials, lack the soft, natural appearance of stone. Concrete, almost without exception, looks too starkly modern. Brick usually seems more suited to the manor house than the cottage, especially when it's precisely set and mortared. For a brick wall with some country character, use bricks of different kinds and sizes; the result will have an irregularity reminiscent of stone walls.

HEDGES Cottagers without a ready supply of stone or wood had one fencing option left: hedge plants. And the denser and thornier, the better—the hedge was to serve as a barrier, after all. Today, though (unless you, too, are attempting to exclude marauding animals!), you can select plants based solely on appearance and density. The best hedges are thickly foliaged types that can be maintained by occasional shearing to restrict height and spread. A relaxed, unclipped look is more in keeping with the cottage spirit than a formally sheared, geometric border.

Fortunate is the homeowner who has access to good building stone—and foolish is the one who doesn't take advantage of it! The higher wall (at left) provides a natural-looking backdrop for a cloak of 'Paul's Scarlet Climber' roses, while the lower one (at right) forms a neat boundary.

GATES

Fences separate two areas, but gates are meant to join them, linking one side with the other. In olden times, they were typically fashioned from whatever was at hand (generally branches or other wood scraps), and function was the primary concern: if the gate opened easily and closed securely, who cared about design? Not so today, though. Form has become almost as important as function. Some gates are whimsical, some are excursions into fine art, and others simply show off expert craftsmanship—in materials that range from scavenged to manufactured.

To narrow down your choices, ask the usual question: "Does it suit the mood?" Take care to avoid anything too tall or solid: a high, impregnable-looking gate signals "keep out" rather than "enter." More suitable are low or open-structured gates that clearly invite the visitor to lift the latch and come through. As for materials, you needn't opt for the deliberately rustic, but do avoid anything too fancy or upscale.

Wrought iron is especially tricky: the plainest designs may fit in nicely, but any veer toward the elaborate will suggest the estate rather than the cottage.

Each situation will call for its own approach. In a wide-open setting, you'll probably want something that stands apart from the surroundings and from the wall on either side. But where the setting is also the jewel, featuring many elements that attract the eye, the better design is one that blends smoothly into the background.

Set into a rough rock wall, this slatted wooden gate is a stable, unpretentious portal, its pickets allowing a glimpse of what lies beyond. Natural materials like stone and unpainted wood merge with the garden more and more as they weather with the years, finally looking as though they'd always been there.

LEFT *Creativity and craftsmanship produce an inviting garden entrance that's also a place to pause and sit a while: the shallow, rose-bedecked arch hovers over—and forms the backs of—two simple wooden benches.* **RIGHT** *A gussied-up version of the basic tripod, this four-legged pyramid supports a thriving gold flame honeysuckle in riotous bloom.*

TRIPODS, ARCHES, AND ARBORS

Tripods, arches, and arbors were originally contrived to support and elevate vining crops, letting them grow without entangling other plants. Nowadays, though, they're largely used for ornamentals; you're more likely to see arches and arbors supporting roses or wisteria, for example, than beans or grapes. The structures themselves are often works of art; even the humble tripod (still a vegetable garden standby) has evolved to include decorative versions more suited to ornamental plants.

The basic *tripod* is simply three poles placed at the corner points of a triangle (or four poles arranged in a square), then angled inward so the top ends meet at a central point. Twining vines wrap around each pole. Upscale versions are garden pyramids made of long-lasting finished lumber—useful for supporting pole beans, for sure, but more likely to be adorned by something more elegant. A variant is the "tower": four vertical poles or posts connected to one another by crosspieces resembling the rungs of a ladder. The plant to be supported grows inside the tower. These structures are especially useful for displaying lax-caned, not-quite-climbing roses.

Slender saplings provided material for the simplest *arches.* The more supple ones could be bent into a hairpin; somewhat less flexible pieces could be bent enough to meet each other, then tied together to form a broader curve. Such structures are perfect for displaying twining vines. To accommodate more growth, two arches can be joined with ladderlike crosspieces to create a structure with some depth, reminiscent of a very shallow tunnel or barrel vault.

An *arbor* is a variant of an arch in which all the curved lines are replaced by straight ones: two vertical members are joined at the top by a horizontal crosspiece. Variations include an expanded version with four uprights and side crosspieces and one with two vertical posts supporting a broad, flat, ladderlike top piece.

LEFT *Outfitted with an arbor—or a row of them, as here—a simple path becomes a shady, semi-enclosed passageway.* **TOP RIGHT** *Lax-caned roses need a strong support such as this basic four-legged plant tower.* **BOTTOM RIGHT** *Carefully crafted double arch is a classic display case for enthusiastic climbers like this lavishly blooming rose.*

Contemporary arches and arbors follow the original designs, but the range of available materials has expanded. The traditional saplings and branches can still be used to create short-lived structures with true country charm, but many gardeners today prefer longer-lasting materials. Finished lumber makes sturdy arches and arbors that can either be painted or just left to weather to a neutral gray. Steel rods and malleable copper tubing are good choices as well; both are unobtrusive, long lasting, and appropriately modest in appearance. Wood and metal can also be combined in attractive designs. And if you're lucky enough to have a supply of natural stone, your arbor can have stone pillars as its vertical supports.

TRELLISES

Another accommodation for vining plants is the trellis, typically a gridwork panel that can be freestanding or mounted on a flat, vertical surface. If wall mounted, it shouldn't form a secondary wall, but simply give vines sufficient "handholds" to keep them securely aloft.

Manufactured latticework, available in panels ready for mounting, is probably the most familiar trellis, but such panels are often rather tightly woven, more suitable for screening than for hosting vines. The ideal trellis has a looser grid, with openings large enough to permit good air circulation and let vines weave in and out if they're so inclined. Most trellises have regular openings (be they squares, rectangles, or diamonds), but there's no reason you can't combine natural materials to form irregular trelliswork. Just make sure the end result is in a relatively flat plane.

Manufactured fan-shaped trellises are also available in wood (by far the better choice for cottage gardens) or plastic. These are typically less sturdy than lattices, making them better suited for relatively small, lightweight vines.

A luxuriant clematis vine engulfs a sturdy trellis, smothering it in a cloud of snowy white blossoms. The widely spaced latticework encourages the vines to wander through from one side to another and allows air to circulate freely around the foliage.

SEATING

Be it a simple plank or a meticulously crafted hardwood seat, a bench in any form offers respite. When you're working in the garden, it lets you take a rest without sitting on the ground; when the job is done, it offers a vantage point for admiring your accomplishments. And at any time, a bench is an invitation simply to sit outdoors and relax.

The wooden bench is a traditional choice, blending beautifully into the garden: left unpainted and allowed to weather, it soon looks as if it had always been there. Stone benches are far less common, partly because good stone is scarcer than wood, partly because they're harder to build.

TOP Nearly swallowed by exuberant plantings, a whimsical garden chair is both functional seating and garden art. **BOTTOM LEFT** *Recycling a patio or lawn chair is in keeping with the old cottage tradition of using the materials at hand.* **BOTTOM RIGHT** *An elegantly simple teak bench beckons visitors, inviting them to sit and contemplate—but it doesn't steal attention from the floral main attractions.*

But if quality construction stone is native to your region of the country, don't hesitate to use it. A stone bench—or one with stone supports and a wooden seat—will look as though it had grown from the earth.

Wrought iron benches reflect an industrial era several centuries beyond the time of the original cottage gardens. Nonetheless, most have a suitably old-fashioned appearance that's entirely compatible with the cottage style.

Cottage garden seating also includes simple chairs. Like benches, they're often built from lumber, but their smaller size also invites creative construction from branches, as the bentwood chair on page 14 shows.

Benches vary to suit the garden. **TOP LEFT** *Just a bit ornate, this white-painted wrought iron bench harmonizes with the graceful wisteria overhead and the window framing nearby.* **CENTER LEFT** *A simple plank bench lets you relax among blooming nasturtiums.* **BOTTOM LEFT** *Old park-style bench offers a nearly hidden resting spot.* **RIGHT** *A durable hardwood bench is just the place for enjoying a cup of tea and a good book.*

CONTAINERS

The first container plant probably wasn't intended to grow in its pot permanently. Instead, the pot was doubtless pressed into service simply for transport. Only when someone noticed that the plant looked good (or, perhaps, grew better) that way did the idea of container gardening come into its own.

Nowadays, almost anything that will hold soil has been pressed into container service—from old baby shoes to claw-foot bathtubs to the trunks of 1960s Detroit convertibles! For a cottage garden, though, the container you use should suit the casual, country atmosphere. Think of what the original cottagers would have had on hand: an old bucket or cooking kettle, a wicker basket, perhaps a terra-cotta pot or stone trough. To preserve the understated cottage charm, keep to simple shapes and natural materials, avoiding anything that appears highly manufactured or overly cute. The most successful containers seem to belong to the garden rather than standing out from it.

Here's a floral act you can take on the road! This jam-packed wheelbarrow may be plainly present-day, but it's entirely in keeping with the cottage spirit: old-time gardeners, too, would have pressed such worn-out "containers" into use as planters.

LEFT *The basic sundial is a model of simplicity: a pedestal supports a flat surface, on which a gnomon casts the shadow that tells the time. Traditional version (top) has circular disk much like a clock face. Square model (bottom) differs only in design, not in function.* **RIGHT** *Held aloft by a bronze figure, an armillary sphere rests atop a pedestal with sculpted decoration that echoes the horticultural tapestry all around.*

SUNDIALS

Sundials are as attractive and useful now as they were centuries ago, before household clocks became affordable and widely available. Usually mounted on a pedestal, the basic sundial is a flat disk marked with the hours; a triangle or obliquely angled arm *(gnomon)* casts a shadow on the disk to indicate the time.

The armillary sphere, also pedestal mounted, is a more complex device featuring a series of intersecting rings that represent the positions of the celestial spheres. Though far from a typical detail of cottage gardens, it definitely adds an appropriate aura of antiquity to a traditional planting.

Resembling a little red barn, this bright bird house rises above a riot of summer annuals, its painted surfaces seemingly an extension of the colorful display below. In a pastel scheme, the same nesting house might be used unpainted: natural wood harmonizes nicely with quieter colors.

BIRD FEEDERS, BATHS, AND HOUSES

Bird-friendly features are perfectly in keeping with the spirit and appearance of a cottage garden. By providing your feathered visitors appropriate food, drink, and shelter, you can both benefit them and give yourself a source of endless entertainment. What's more, many birds can help you keep the garden healthy and luxuriant by controlling a variety of insect pests.

When considering feeders, baths, and houses, keep simplicity in mind. Elaborate "apartment" housing, for instance, may be attractive in the catalog, but in a cottage garden it will seem overdone. As usual, look for plain designs and natural materials. Unfinished, naturally weathered wood makes fine houses and feeders. Ceramic, either glazed or unglazed, serves well for birdbaths.

Above all, make sure the amenities you provide really will encourage birds to visit. Positioning is critical, since birds tend to avoid areas that they sense will leave them vulnerable to predators.

Also be aware that "if you build it, they will come" doesn't always hold true for housing.

Different species of birds have differing and quite specific requirements for the height of the house above the ground, its location, the size and placement of its "door," and so on. For details on all these points, consult Sunset's *Building Birdhouses*.

White sweet alyssum and pink perennial pincushion flowers frame a simple birdbath with a glazed interior. The ceramic bird in the center has more than a decorative function: real birds waiting their turn in the water—or those drying off—can use it as a perch.

A gazing globe is a simple artistic addition that creates an instant focal point. Its polished surface shines and glitters, offering a curving, interestingly altered reflection of sky and garden. Available in many colors, globes can complement garden color schemes (as this one does) or contrast with them.

GARDEN ART

The earliest, working cottage gardens were doubtless devoid of art as we know it. Garden tools left leaning against a wall may have created a casually artistic composition purely by chance, but those shovels, hoes, rakes, and scythes were hardly intended as adornment.

Still, that original lack of deliberate garden art is no reason to restrict or scuttle your decorative impulses. Just bear in mind that plants are the stars of any cottage garden—so if you do include art, it should not overwhelm the space or clash with the overall style.

As a rule of thumb, keep artistic touches simple, fairly

understated, and, as always, appropriate. Steer clear of the ultra-modern, abstract sculpture that's at odds with the garden's casual, countrified atmosphere; also avoid deliberately rustic appurtenances such as the plaster goose girl trailed by her plaster flock or the cutie-pie concrete lad bearing a fishing pole and bait bucket.

None of these cautions rules out something as eye-catching as a metal moose, for example (see the photograph below). If you're inclined toward such potentially show-off pieces, however, the trick is to nestle them into the plantings, making them part of the ensemble rather than a stand-out detail.

LEFT *Is it art or a container-in-waiting? The question is part of this classic urn's appeal.* **TOP RIGHT** *No one would challenge a sunflower in a cottage garden, so a whimsical metallic replica is an appropriate accent.* **BOTTOM RIGHT** *The horticultural equivalent of a bull in a china shop, this rusty iron moose seems poised to plow through a drift of nasturtiums.*

SUNSET'S GARDEN CLIMATE ZONES

A plant's performance is governed by the total climate: length of growing season, timing and amount of rainfall, winter lows, summer highs, humidity. *Sunset*'s climate zone maps take all these factors into account—unlike the familiar hardiness zone maps devised by the U.S. Department of Agriculture, which divide the U.S. and Canada into zones based strictly on winter lows. The U.S.D.A. maps tell you only where a plant may survive the winter; our climate zone maps let you see where that plant will thrive year-round. Below and on page 188 are brief descriptions of the zones illustrated on the maps on pages 186–188. For more information, consult *Sunset*'s regional garden books.

ZONE 1A. Coldest Mountain and Intermountain Areas in the West

All zone is west of Continental Divide. Growing season mid-June to early September, with mild days, chilly nights. Average lows to −0°F/−18°C, extreme lows to −40F/−40C; snow cover (or winter mulch) key to perennials success.

ZONE 1B. Coldest Eastern Rockies and Plains Climate

All zone is east of Continental Divide. Growing season mid-May to late September: warm days, warmer nights than 1A. Summer rainfall present, wind a constant. Winter Arctic cold fronts create sudden temperature shifts; average lows to 0°F/−18°C, extreme lows to −50°F/−46°C.

ZONE 2A. Cold Mountain and Intermountain Areas

Growing season mid-May to mid-September. Occurs at lower elevation than Zone 1A; summers are mild, winters to 10°F/−12°C (extremes to −30°F/−34°C) with snow. The coldest zone for growing sweet cherries, hardiest apples.

ZONE 2B. Warmer-Summer Intermountain Climate

Growing season mid-May to October. Premier fruit- and grain-growing climate with long, warm to hot summers. Winters to 12°F/−11°C (extremes to −20°F/−23°C) with snow.

ZONE 3A. Mild Areas of Mountain and Intermountain Climates

Growing season May to mid-October. Long, dry, warm summers favor a variety of warm-season crops, deciduous fruits, many ornamentals. Occurs at higher elevation the farther south it is found. Winter temperatures drop to 15°F/−9°C with extremes to −18°F/-28°C; snow is possible.

ZONE 3B. Mildest Areas on Intermountain Climates

Growing season early April to late October. Compared to Zone 3A, summers are warmer, winters milder: to 19°F/-7°C with extremes to −15°F/−26°C. Snow is possible. Excellent climate for vegetables, also a wide variety of ornamentals that prefer dry atmosphere.

ZONE 4. Cold-winter Western Washington and British Columbia

Growing season: early May to early Oct. Summers are cool, thanks to ocean influence; chilly winters (19° to −7°F/−7° to −22°C) result from elevation, influence of continental air mass, or both. Coolness, ample rain suit many perennials and bulbs.

ZONE 5. Ocean-influenced Northwest Coast and Puget Sound

Growing season: mid-April to Nov., typically with cool temperatures throughout. Less rain falls here than in Zone 4; winter lows range from 28° to 1°F/−2° to −17°C. This "English garden" climate is ideal for rhododendrons and many rock garden plants.

ZONE 6. Oregon's Willamette Valley

Growing season: mid-Mar. to mid-Nov., with somewhat warmer temperatures than in Zone 5. Ocean influence keeps winter lows about the same as in Zone 5. Climate suits all but tender plants and those needing hot or dry summers.

ZONE 7. Oregon's Rogue River Valley, California's High Foothills

Growing season: May to early Oct. Summers are hot and dry; typical winter lows run from 23° to 9°F/−5° to −13°C. The summer-winter contrast suits plants that need dry, hot summers and moist, only moderately cold winters.

ZONE 8. Cold-air Basins of California's Central Valley

Growing season: mid-Feb. through Nov. This is a valley floor with no maritime influence. Summers are hot; winter lows range from 29° to 13°F/−2° to −11°C. Rain comes in the cooler months, covering just the early part of the growing season.

ZONE 9. Thermal Belts of California's Central Valley

Growing season: late Feb. through Dec. Zone 9 is located in the higher elevations around Zone 8, but its summers are just as hot; its winter lows are slightly higher (temperatures range from 28° to 18°F/−2° to −8°C). Rainfall pattern is the same as in Zone 8.

ZONE 10. High Desert Areas of Arizona, New Mexico, West Texas, Oklahoma Panhandle, and Southwest Kansas

Growing season: April to early Nov. Chilly (even snow-dusted) weather rules from late Nov. through Feb., with lows from 31° to 24°F/−1° to −4°C. Rain comes in summer as well as in the cooler seasons.

ZONE 11. Medium to High Desert of California and Southern Nevada

Growing season: early April to late Oct. Summers are sizzling, with 110 days above 90°F/32°C. Balancing this is a 3½-month winter, with 85 nights below freezing and lows from 11° to 0°F/−12° to −18°C. Scant rainfall comes in winter.

ZONE 12. Arizona's Intermediate Desert

Growing season: mid-Mar. to late Nov., with scorching midsummer heat. Compared to Zone 13, this region has harder frosts; record low is 6°F/−14°C. Rains come in summer and winter.

ZONE 13. Low or Subtropical Desert

Growing season: mid-Feb. through Nov., interrupted by nearly 3 months of incandescent, growth-stopping summer heat. Most frosts are light (record lows run from 19° to 13°F/−17° to −11°C); scant rain comes in summer and winter.

ZONE 14. Inland Northern and Central California with Some Ocean Influence

Growing season: early Mar. to mid-Nov., with rain coming in the remaining months. Periodic intrusions of marine air temper summer heat and winter cold (lows run from 26° to 16°F/−3° to −9°C). Mediterranean-climate plants are at home here.

ZONE 15. Northern and Central California's Chilly-winter Coast-influenced Areas

Growing season: Mar. to Dec. Rain comes from fall through winter. Typical winter lows range from 28° to 21°F/−2° to −6°C. Maritime air influences the zone much of the time, giving it cooler, moister summers than Zone 14.

ZONE 16. Northern and Central California Coast Range Thermal Belts

Growing season: late Feb. to late Nov. With cold air draining to lower elevations, winter lows typically run from 32° to 19°F/0° to −7°C. Like Zone 15, this region is dominated by maritime air, but its winters are milder on average.

ZONE 17. Oceanside Northern and Central California and Southernmost Oregon

Growing season: late Feb. to early Dec. Coolness and fog are hallmarks; summer highs seldom top 75°F/24°C, while winter lows run from 36° to 23°F/2° to −5°C. Heat-loving plants disappoint or dwindle here.

ZONE 18. Hilltops and Valley Floors of Interior Southern California

Growing season: mid-Mar. through late Nov. Summers are hot and dry; rain comes in winter, when lows reach 28° to 10°F/–2° to –12°C. Plants from the Mediterranean and Near Eastern regions thrive here.

ZONE 19. Thermal belts around Southern California's Interior Valleys

Growing season: early Mar. through Nov. As in Zone 18, rainy winters and hot, dry summers are the norm—but here, winter lows dip only to 27° to 22°F/–3° to –6°C, allowing some tender evergreen plants to grow outdoors with protection.

ZONE 20. Hilltops and Valley Floors of Ocean-influenced Inland Southern California

Growing season: late Mar. to late Nov.—but fairly mild winters (lows of 28° to 23°F/–2° to –5°C) allow gardening through much of the year. Cool and moist maritime influence alternates with hot, dry interior air.

ZONE 21. Thermal Belts around Southern California's Ocean-influenced Interior Valleys

Growing season: early Mar. to early Dec., with same tradeoff of oceanic and interior influence as in Zone 20. During winter rainy season, lows range from 36° to 23°F/2° to –5°C—warmer than Zone 20, since colder air drains to the valleys.

ZONE 22. Colder-winter Parts of Southern California's Coastal Region

Growing season: Mar. to early Dec. Winter lows seldom fall below 28°F/–2°C (records are around 21°F/–6°C), though colder air sinks to this zone from Zone 23. Summers are warm; rain comes in winter. Climate here is largely oceanic.

ZONE 23. Thermal Belts of Southern California's Coastal Region

Growing season: almost year-round (all but first half of Jan.). Rain comes in winter. Reliable ocean influence keeps summers mild (except when hot Santa Ana winds come from inland), frosts negligible; 23°F/–5°C is the record low.

ZONE 24. Marine-dominated Southern California Coast

Growing season: all year, but periodic freezes have dramatic effects (record lows are 33° to 20°F/1° to –7°C). Climate here is oceanic (but warmer than oceanic Zone 17), with cool summers, mild winters. Subtropical plants thrive.

ZONE 25. South Florida and the Keys

Growing season: all year. Add ample year-round rainfall (least in Dec. through Mar.), high humidity, and overall warmth, and you have a near-tropical climate. The Keys are frost-free; winter lows elsewhere run from 40° to 25°F/4° to –4°C.

ZONE 26. Central and Interior Florida

Growing season: early Feb. to late Dec., with typically humid, warm to hot weather. Rain is plentiful all year, heaviest in summer and early fall. Lows range from 15°F/–9°C in the north to 27°F/–3°C in the south; arctic air brings periodic hard freezes.

ZONE 27. Lower Rio Grande Valley

Growing season: early Mar. to mid-Dec.. Summers are hot and humid; winter lows only rarely dip below freezing. Many plants from tropical and subtropical Africa and South America are well adapted here.

ZONE 28. Gulf Coast, North Florida, Atlantic Coast to Charleston

Growing season: mid-Mar. to early Dec. Humidity and rainfall are year-round phenomena; summers are hot, winters virtually frostless but subject to periodic invasions by frigid arctic air. Azaleas, camellias, many subtropicals flourish.

ZONE 29. Interior Plains of South Texas

Growing season: mid-Mar. through Nov. Moderate rainfall (to 25" annually) comes year-round. Summers are hot. Winter lows can dip to 26°F/–3°C, with occasional arctic freezes bringing much lower readings.

ZONE 30. Hill Country of Central Texas

Growing season: mid-Mar. through Nov. Zone 30 has higher annual rainfall than Zone 29 (to 35") and lower winter temperatures, normally to around 20°F/–7°C. Seasonal variations favor many fruit crops, perennials.

ZONE 31. Interior Plains of Gulf Coast and Coastal Southeast

Growing season: mid-Mar. to early Nov. In this extensive east-west zone, hot and sticky summers contrast with chilly winters (record low temperatures are 7° to 0°F/–14° to –18°C). There's rain all year (an annual average of 50"), with the least falling in Oct.

ZONE 32. Interior Plains of Mid-Atlantic States; Chesapeake Bay, Southeastern Pennsylvania, Southern New Jersey

Growing season: late Mar. to early Nov. Rain falls year-round (40" to 50" annually); winter lows (moving through the zone from south to north) are 30° to 20°F/–1° to –7°C. Humidity is less oppressive here than in Zone 31.

ZONE 33. North-Central Texas and Oklahoma Eastward to the Appalachian Foothills

Growing season: mid-April through Oct. Warm Gulf Coast air and colder continental/arctic fronts both play a role; their unpredictable interplay results in a wide range in annual rainfall (22" to 52") and winter lows (20° to 0°F/–7° to –18°C). Summers are muggy and warm to hot.

ZONE 34. Lowlands and Coast from Gettysburg to North of Boston

Growing season: late April to late Oct. Ample rainfall and humid summers are the norm. Winters are variable—typically fairly mild (around 20°F/–7°C), but with lows down to –3° to –22°F/–19° to –30°C if arctic air swoops in.

ZONE 35. Ouachita Mountains, Northern Oklahoma and Arkansas, Southern Kansas to North-Central Kentucky and Southern Ohio

Growing season: late April to late Oct. Rain comes in all seasons. Summers can be truly hot and humid. Without arctic fronts, winter lows are around 18°F/–8°C; with them, the coldest weather may bring lows of –20°F/–29°C.

ZONE 36. Appalachian Mountains

Growing season: May to late Oct. Thanks to greater elevation, summers are cooler and less humid, winters colder (0° to –20°F/–18° to –29°C) than in adjacent, lower zones. Rain comes all year (heaviest in spring). Late frosts are common.

ZONE 37. Hudson Valley and Appalachian Plateau

Growing season: May to mid-Oct., with rainfall throughout. Lower in elevation than neighboring Zone 42, with warmer winters: lows are 0° to –5°F/–18° to –21°C, unless arctic air moves in. Summer is warm to hot, humid.

ZONE 38. New England Interior and Lowland Maine

Growing season: May to early Oct. Summers feature reliable rainfall and lack oppressive humidity of lower-elevation, more southerly areas. Winter lows dip to –10° to –20°F/–23° to –29°C, with periodic colder temperatures due to influxes of arctic air.

ZONE 39. Shoreline Regions of the Great Lakes

Growing season: early May to early Oct. Springs and summers are cooler here, autumns milder than in areas farther from the lakes. Southeast lakeshores get the heaviest snowfalls. Lows reach 0° to –10°F/–18° to –23°C.

ZONE 40. Inland Plains of Lake Erie and Lake Ontario

Growing season: mid-May to mid-Sept., with rainy, warm, variably humid weather. The lakes help moderate winter lows; temperatures typically range from –10° to –20°F/–23° to –29°C, with occasional colder readings when arctic fronts rush through.

Sunset's Garden Climate Zones

Climate Zones	⫽	1A	1B	2A	2B	3A	3B	4	5	6	7	8	9	10	11	12	13	14	15	16	17	18	19	20	21	22

27

James
Bay

45

ONTARIO

QUÉBEC

NEW
BRUNSWICK

44

45

43

Québec

Presque
Isle

Lake
of the
Woods

Lake
Superior

43

42

MAINE

38

MINNESOTA

45

MICHIGAN

43

Montréal

Bangor

Duluth

35

Ottawa

St. Lawrence River

95

94

43

VERMONT

Portland

Minneapolis

94

WISCONSIN

Lake
Huron

43

Burlington

43

42

NEW
HAMPSHIRE

38

43

MICHIGAN

40

87

1

38

Toronto

Lake
Ontario

39

Boston

90

43

Lake
Michigan

41

75

43

Albany

88

91

MASSACHUSETTS

43

Milwaukee

39

40

Buffalo

81

90

87

37

34

RHODE ISLAND

90

94

90

Detroit

Lake
Erie

90

NEW YORK

81

CONNECTICUT

34

Dubuque

41

Chicago

519

94

39

Cleveland

80

90

42

Newark

95

New
York

35

IOWA

80

80

80

Akron

71

79

PENNSYLVANIA

78

40

Des
Moines

80

55

75

77

80

Philadelphia

NEW
JERSEY

74

65

69

OHIO

41

Pittsburgh

76

34

57

Columbus

70

DELAWARE

32

29

41

Springfield

INDIANA

71

79

36

66

Washington,
D.C.

35

ILLINOIS

Indianapolis

70

Cincinnati

WEST
VIRGINIA

95

MARYLAND

Missouri River

55

65

35

79

Charleston

64

Richmond

Kansas
City

70

St.
Louis

70

35

Louisville

64

VIRGINIA

44

57

Ohio River

75

81

32

85

31

MISSOURI

44

65

KENTUCKY

36

95

Atlantic
Ocean

35

77

Raleigh

Nashville

40

85

MISSISSIPPI River

33

TENNESSEE

24

75

NORTH
CAROLINA

40

ARKANSAS

40

33

32

31

Arkansas River

Memphis

SOUTH
CAROLINA

95

Little
Rock

35

65

85

32

Columbia

Red River

30

59

26

33

55

Atlanta

20

30

Birmingham

59

GEORGIA

ALABAMA

85

16

Shreveport

20

MISSISSIPPI

65

75

31

Savannah

LOUISIANA

Jackson

59

0   100   200   300 miles

49

31

28

Lake
Pontchartrain

10

Jacksonville

10

Mobile

10

75

95

Houston

28

New
Orleans

45

FLORIDA

Gulf of
Mexico

Orlando

4

Tampa

26

75

Lake
Okeechobee

25

Miami

© 2001 Sunset Books Inc. All rights rese

rved.

| 23 | 24 | 25 | 26 | 27 | 28 | 29 | 30 | 31 | 32 | 33 | 34 | 35 | 36 | 37 | 38 | 39 | 40 | 41 | 42 | 43 | 44 | 45 | Climate Zones |

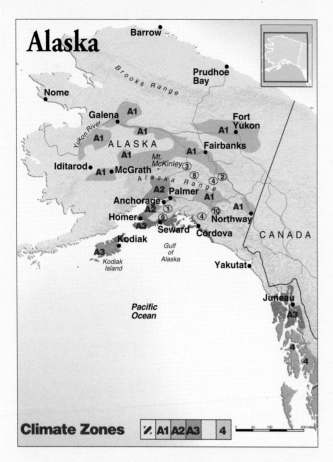

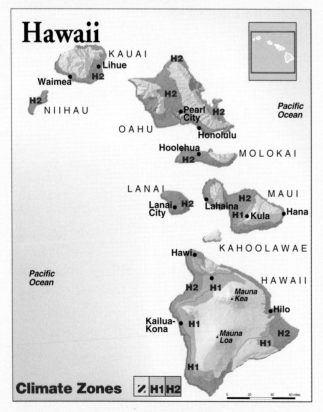

ZONE 41. Northeast Kansas and Southeast Nebraska to Northern Illinois and Indiana, Southeast Wisconsin, Michigan, Northern Ohio

Growing season: early May to early Oct. Winter brings average lows of −11° to −20°F/−23° to −29°C. Summers in this zone are hotter and longer west of the Mississippi, cooler and shorter nearer the Great Lakes; summer rainfall increases in the same west-to-east direction.

ZONE 42. Interior Pennsylvania and New York; St. Lawrence Valley

Growing season: late May to late Sept. This zone's elevation gives it colder winters than surrounding zones: lows range from −20° to −40°F/−29° to −40°C, with the colder readings coming in the Canadian portion of the zone. Summers are humid, rainy.

ZONE 43. Upper Mississippi Valley, Upper Michigan, Southern Ontario and Quebec

Growing season: late May to mid-Sept. The climate is humid from spring through early fall; summer rains are usually dependable. Arctic air dominates in winter, with lows typically from −20° to −30°F/−29° to −34°C.

ZONE 44. Mountains of New England and Southeastern Quebec

Growing season: June to mid-Sept. Latitude and elevation give fairly cool, rainy summers, cold winters with lows of −20° to −40°F/−29° to −40°C. Choose short-season, low heat-requirement annuals and vegetables.

ZONE 45. Northern Parts of Minnesota and Wisconsin, Eastern Manitoba through Interior Quebec

Growing season: mid-June through Aug., with rain throughout; rainfall (and humidity) are least in zone's western part, greatest in eastern reaches. Winters are frigid (−30° to −40°F/−34° to −40°C), with snow cover, deeply frozen soil.

ZONE A1. Alaska's Coldest Climate—Fairbanks and the Interior

Growing season mid-May to early September. Summer days are long, mild to warm; permafrost usually recedes below root zone. Winter offers reliable snow cover. Season extenders include planting in south and west exposures, boosting soil temperature with mulches or IRT plastic sheeting. Winter lows drop to −20°F/−29°C, with occasional extremes to −60°F/−51°C.

ZONE A2. The Intermediate Climate of Anchorage and Cook Inlet

Growing season mid-May to mid-September. Climate is moderated by mountains to the north and south, also by water of Cook Inlet. Microclimates reign supreme: winter lows may be 5°F/−15°C but with extremes of −40°F/−40°C possible. Summer days are cool to mild and frequently cloudy.

ZONE A3. Mild Southern Maritime Climate from Kodiak to Juneau

Growing season mid-May to October. Summers are cool and cloudy, winters rainy and windy. Typical lows are to 18°F/−8°C with extremes to −18°F/−28°C. Winter-spring freeze-thaw cycles damage plants that break growth early. Cool-weather plants revel in climate but annual types mature more slowly than usual.

ZONE H1. Cooler Volcanic Slopes from 2,000 to 5,000 Feet Elevation

Found only on Hawaii and Maui, this zone offers cooler air (and cooler nights) than lower Zone H2; temperatures here are better for low-chill fruits (especially at higher elevations) and many non-tropical ornamentals. Warm-season highs reach 65° to 80°F/19° to 27°C; cool-season lows drop to around 45°F/7°C.

ZONE H2. Sea Level to 2,000 Feet: the Coconut Palm Belt

The most heavily populated region in the islands, this has tepid climate with high temperatures in the 80° to 90°F/27° to 32°C range, low temperatures only to about 65°F/18°C. Rainiest period is November through March, the remaining months, on leeward sides, being relatively dry. Windward sides of islands get more precipitation than leeward sides from passing storms and year-round tradewind showers.

INDEX

A

Achillea, 7, 16, 20, 31, 32, 34, 35, 36, 37, 52
Agastache, 31, 32, 34, 35, 36, 37, 52–53
Alcea, 19, 32, 34, 35, 39, 50, 67
Althaea, shrub, See *Hibiscus*
Anemone, 31
Angel hair, See *Artemisia*
Annuals, 31, 42–49, 70–71
Antirrhinum, 34, 35, 42
Apple, See *Malus*
Aquilegia, 5, 31, 33, 34, 39, 53
Artemisia, 7, 31, 36, 80
Artichoke, 89
Asclepias, 31, 34, 35, 36, 37, 53
Asparagus, 89
Aster, 32, 34, 54
Aurinia, 32, 36, 54

B

Baby's breath, See *Gypsophila*
Bachelor's button, See *Centaurea*
Basil, See *Ocimum*
Basket-of-gold, See *Aurinia*
Beans, 10, 90
Beauty bush, See *Kolkwitzia*
Beds, 27, 28, 32, 35, 37, 38
Bellflower, See *Campanula*
Betony, wood, See *Stachys*
Biennials, 31, 50–51
Bindweed, See *Convolvulus*
Black-eyed Susan, See *Rudbeckia*
Blue mist, See *Caryopteris*
Blue oat grass, See *Helictotrichon*
Bluebell, See *Campanula*
Boltonia, 14
Buddleja, 31, 33, 34, 66
Bull grass, See *Muhlenbergia*
Butterflies, 34–35
Butterfly bush, See *Buddleja*
Butterfly weed, See *Asclepias*

C

Cabbage, 90
Calamagrostis, 85
Calendula, 33, 35, 36, 42
Calliopsis, See *Coreopsis*
Campanula, 14, 32, 50–51, 54–55
Campion, rose, See *Lychnis*
Candytuft, evergreen, See *Iberis*
Canterbury bells, See *Campanula*
Carnation, See *Dianthus*
Caryopteris, 31, 32, 34, 36, 37, 66
Catmint, See *Nepeta*
Centaurea, 33, 36, 42–43, 44
Centranthus, 31, 34, 35, 36, 55
Cercis, 74
Cherry, flowering, See *Prunus*
Chives, 31, 90–91
Chrysanthemum, 16, 32, 34, 35, 55–56
Clary, annual, See *Salvia*
Clematis, 10, 31, 71–72, 113

Cleome, 7, 21, 31, 32, 34, 35, 43
Climate, 13, 16, 17–21
Color, 10, 28, 45
Columbine, See *Aquilegia*
Coneflower, purple, See *Echinacea*
Consolida, 34, 43
Convolvulus, 36
Coral bells, See *Heuchera*
Coreopsis, 31, 33, 35, 36, 37, 43
Cornflower, See *Centaurea*
Cornus, 31, 33, 74, 104
Cosmos, 31, 33, 35, 36, 44
Cottage garden
    contemporary, 11, 85
    English estate gardens, 9, 10
    the essence, 8–9, 11
    historical background, 6–8
    traditional, 6, 8–9, 10–11, 13
Cotton, lavender, See *Santolina*
Cowslip, See *Primula*
Crabapple, See *Malus*
Cranesbill, See *Geranium*
Crape myrtle, See *Lagerstroemia*
Crataegus, 33, 36, 74–75

D

Daisy, See *Aster; Chrysanthemum*
Daylily, See *Hemerocallis*
Delphinium, See *Consolida; Delphinium*
Delphinium, 6, 14, 32, 34, 39, 56, 61
Deschampsia, 85
Design, 24–27, 29
Details and accessories
    arbors, 10, 25, 29, 111–112
    arches, 108, 111–112
    birdbaths and feeders, 103, 106, 118–119
    containers, 10, 11, 25, 116
    garden art, 114, 120–121
    gates, 29, 30, 110
    pergolas, 25, 29
    seating, 10, 14, 25, 111, 114–115
    sundials, 11, 117
    trellises, 10, 113
    tripods, 111
Deutzia, 31, 66
Dianthus, 5, 7, 20, 32, 33, 34, 35, 50–51, 56–57
Digitalis, 19, 31, 33, 34, 51, 69
Dogwood, See *Cornus*
Dolichos, 90
Drought-tolerant plants, 36–37, 105

E

Echinacea, 31, 33, 34, 35, 36, 37, 57
Eggplant, 31, 91
Erysimum, 31, 33, 34, 51
Eschscholzia, 33, 36, 44
Eulalia, See *Miscanthus*
Euphorbia, 32, 37, 57–58

F

Feather reed grass, See *Calamagrostis*
Fennel, See *Foeniculum*
Fescue, See *Festuca*
Festuca, 37, 85–86
Feverfew, See *Chrysanthemum*
Foeniculum, 32, 36, 80–81
Forget-me-not, See *Myosotis*
Fountain grass, See *Pennisetum*
Foxglove, See *Digitalis*
Fruits, *See* Vegetables and fruits

G

Gayfeather, See *Liatris*
Geranium, See *Geranium; Pelargonium*
Geranium, 8, 18, 31, 32, 58
Germander, See *Teucrium*
Giant feather grass, See *Stipa*
Globe amaranth, See *Gomphrena*
Gomphrena, 31, 44
Grape, See *Vitis*
Grasses
    ornamental, 14, 27, 31, 85–88
    turf, 11, 107
Gypsophila, 32, 36, 58–59

H

Hair grass, See *Deschampsia*
Hakonechloa, 86
Hawthorn, See *Crataegus*
Heal-all, See *Prunella*
Heat-tolerant plants, 31
Helianthus, 8, 31, 33, 93
Helictotrichon, 86
Hemerocallis, 21, 59
Herb-of-grace, See *Ruta*
Herbs, 31, 80–84
Heuchera, 32, 34, 35, 59–60
Hibiscus, 31, 34, 37, 67
Hollyhock, See *Alcea*
Honeysuckle, See *Lonicera*
Hyssop, See *Agastache; Hyssopus*
Hyssopus, 31, 52, 81

I

Iberis, 33, 34, 35, 60
Imperata, 86
Ipomoea, 34, 70
Iris, 5, 13, 32, 33, 60–61
Irrigation, 38

J

Japanese blood grass, See *Imperata*
Japanese forest grass, See *Hakonechloa*
Japanese silver grass, See *Miscanthus*
Johnny jump-up, See *Viola*
Jupiter's beard, See *Centranthus*

K

Kale, 90
Kolkwitzia, 31, 34, 67

L

Lagerstroemia, 31, 36, 75
Lamb's ears, See Stachys
Larkspur, See Consolida
Lathyrus, 33, 34, 70–71
Lavandula, 8, 16, 32, 33, 34, 36, 37, 81–82
Lavender, See Lavandula
Lavender cotton, See Santolina
Liatris, 34, 35, 61
Lilac, See Syringa
Lobularia, 32, 33, 34, 35, 45, 119
Lonicera, 31, 33, 34, 36, 72, 111
Love-in-a-mist, See Nigella
Lupine, See Lupinus
Lupinus, 14, 32, 34, 61–62
Lychnis, 31, 32, 36, 62

M

Magnolia, 31, 75–76
Maintenance, 23, 26, 27, 38–39
Maltese cross, See Lychnis
Malus, 74, 76
Marigold, pot, See Calendula
Marjoram, See Origanum
Mignonette, See Reseda
Mint, Korean hummingbird, See Agastache
Miscanthus, 87
Mock orange, See Philadelphus
Molinia, 87
Moor grass, See Molinia
Morning glory, See Convolvulus; Ipomoea
Mother-of-thyme, See Thymus
Mourning bride, See Scabiosa
Mugwort, white, See Artemisia
Muhlenbergia, 31, 36, 87
Muhly, See Muhlenbergia
Myosotis, 31, 45
Myrtle, crape, See Lagerstroemia

N

Nasturtium, See Tropaeolum
Nepeta, 36, 37, 82
Nicotiana, 33, 34, 35, 45–46
Nigella, 31, 33, 46

O

Ocimum basilicum, 82
Orange, mock, See Philadelphus
Oregano, See Origanum
Origanum, 36, 82–83
Ornamental grasses, See under Grasses

P

Paeonia, 12, 19, 32, 33, 39, 62
Panicum, 31, 36, 88
Pansy, See Viola
Papaver, 20, 46–47
Pathways
   about, 9, 104–106
   and maintenance, 26, 27
   planning, 26
   as transition, 25, 108
   width, 26, 27, 104–105
Peach, 91

Pear, See Pyrus
Pennisetum, 14, 36, 37, 88
Penstemon, 14, 34, 35, 63
Peony, See Paeonia
Pepper, 31, 91–92
Perennials, 13, 18, 31, 39, 52–65
Phaseolus, 90
Philadelphus, 33, 34, 67
Phlomis, 31, 36, 67–68
Pincushion flower, See Scabiosa
Pink, See Dianthus; Lychnis
Planning, 24–27, 29
Plant combinations, 27, 28
Plant selection, 13, 27, 28
Plum, flowering, See Prunus
Poppy, See Eschscholzia; Papaver
Portulaca, 31, 36, 47
Primrose, See Primula
Primula, 31, 33, 63
Prunella, 31, 83
Pruning, 39
Prunus, 33, 74, 76–77
Pyrus, 36, 74, 77

R

Redbud, Eastern, See Cercis
Reseda, 33, 47
Rhubarb, 92
Rosa, 16, 19
   bush, 96–101
   centifolia, 98
   China, 99
   and climate, 14, 18, 94
   climbing, 10, 13, 79, 94–96, 109, 111,
      112
   damask, 98, 99
   floribunda, 100
   gallica, 98
   hardy, 101
   hybrid, 94–95, 101
   miniature, 100
   modern, 96, 99–101
   moss, 98–99
   musk, 101
   Noisette, 95
   old, 95–96, 98–99
   repeat-flowering bush, 99–101
   repeat-flowering climbers, 95–96
   in sample garden plans, 32, 33
   shrub, 100–101
   species, 94, 97
   spring-flowering bush, 97–99
   spring-flowering climbers, 94–95
   tea, 95, 99
   trademarked groups, 101
Rose, See Rosa
Rose campion, See Lychnis
Rose moss, See Portulaca
Rose of Sharon, See Hibiscus
Rudbeckia, 20
Rue, See Ruta
Ruta, 83

S

Sage, See Phlomis; Salvia
Salvia, 31, 34, 35, 47–48, 64
Sample gardens, 32, 35, 37
Santolina, 31, 36, 83–84
Scabiosa, 32, 33, 34, 35, 37, 48, 64, 119
Sedum, 32, 35, 64–65
Self-heal, See Prunella
Shade-tolerant plants, 31
Shrub althaea, See Hibiscus
Shrubs, 27, 31, 39, 66–69
Snapdragon, See Antirrhinum
Snowball, Japanese, See Viburnum
Southernwood, See Artemisia
Spider flower, See Cleome
Spiraea, 31, 32, 34, 68
Spurge, See Euphorbia
Stachys, 7, 16, 31, 32, 36, 37, 65
Stipa, 36, 88
Stonecrop, See Sedum
Sunflower, See Helianthus
Sweet alyssum, See Lobularia
Sweet pea, See Lathyrus
Sweet William, See Dianthus
Swiss chard, 93
Switch grass, See Panicum
Syringa, 32, 33, 34, 68–69

T

Temperature, 15–16, 20–21
Teucrium, 31, 36, 84
Thyme, See Thymus
Thymus, 36, 84
Traditional elements, 6, 8–9, 10–11, 13
Trees, 27, 31, 39, 74–77
Tropaeolum, 31, 34, 48, 71, 115
Tufted hair grass, See Deschampsia

V

Valerian, See Centranthus
Vegetables and fruits, 6, 31, 76–77, 89–93
Verbena, 31, 34, 36, 37, 48–49
Viburnum, 31, 33, 69
Vines, 27, 31, 70–73, 111
Viola, 31, 33, 49, 65
Violet, sweet, See Viola
Vitis, 10, 31, 33, 72–73

W

Wallflower, See Erysimum
Walls and fences, 26, 29, 107–109
Washington thorn, See Crataegus
Weigela, 31, 34, 69
Wisteria, 10, 31, 33, 36, 73, 115
Wood betony, See Stachys
Wormwood, See Artemisia

Y

Yarrow, See Achillea

Z

Zucchini, 93